Cable Knitting Stitch Dictionary

A DAVID AND CHARLES BOOK
© Quarto Publishing plc 2024

David and Charles is an imprint of
David and Charles, Ltd, Suite A, Tourism House,
Pynes Hill, Exeter, EX2 5WS

Conceived, edited, and designed by Quarto Publishing,
an imprint of The Quarto Group, 1 Triptych Place,
London, SE1 9SH

First published in the UK and USA in 2024

Debbie Tomkies has asserted her right to be identified
as author of this work in accordance with the
Copyright, Designs and Patents Act, 1988.

The author and publisher have made every effort to
ensure that all the instructions in the book are accurate
and safe, and therefore cannot accept liability for any
resulting injury, damage, or loss to persons or property,
however it may arise.

Names of manufacturers and product ranges are
provided for the information of readers, with no
intention to infringe copyright or trademarks.

A catalogue record for this book is available from the
British Library.

ISBN-13: 9781446312858 paperback
ISBN-13: 9781446312865 EPUB

This book has been printed on paper from
approved suppliers and made from pulp from
sustainable sources.

Printed in China.

10 9 8 7 6 5 4 3 2 1

Editor: Charlene Fernandes
Designer: Eliana Holder
Pattern checker: Julia Hewitt
Copy editor: Katie Hardwicke
Designer (layout): Clare Barber
Art director: Martina Calvio
Photography: Pete Tomkies (swatches),
Nicki Dowey (beauty shots)
Publisher: Lorraine Dickey

David and Charles publishes high-quality books on
a wide range of subjects. For more information visit
www.davidandcharles.com.

Follow us on Instagram by searching for @dandcbooks.

Layout of the digital edition of this book may vary
depending on reader hardware and display settings.

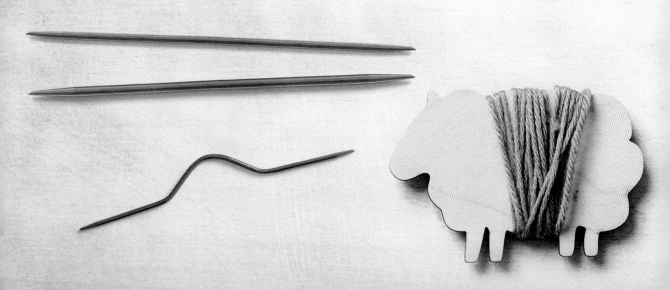

Cable Knitting Stitch Dictionary

Debbie Tomkies

100 ESSENTIAL STITCHES
plus actual-size
swatches and charts

DAVID & CHARLES

www.davidandcharles.com

Contents

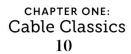

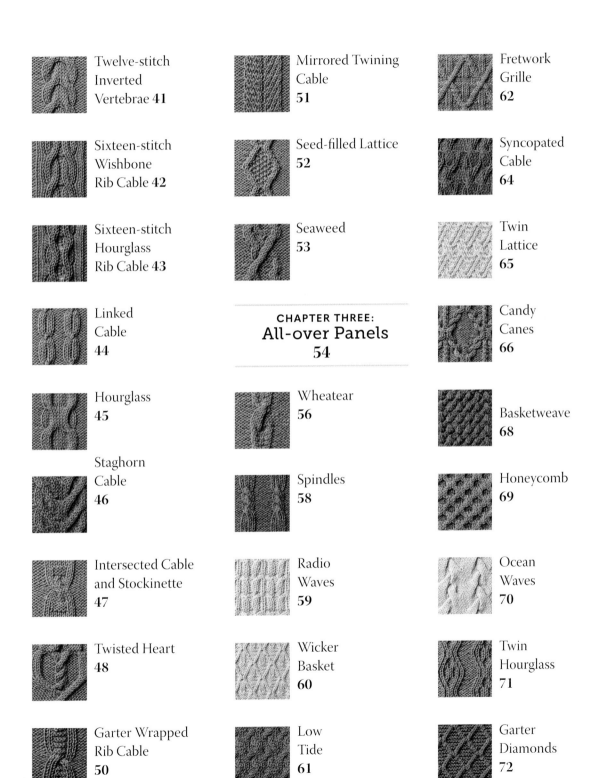

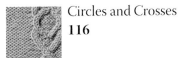
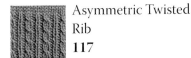

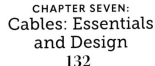

CHAPTER SEVEN:
Cables: Essentials and Design
132

About this book

From an elegant, single rope to a complex honeycomb or braid, incorporating twisted and traveling stitches is a great way to add texture and give structure to a garment.

Cables are essentially combinations of knit and purl stitches worked out of sequence. They can be created in an endless variety of sizes and combinations. Cables are frequently worked in knit stitches on a reverse stockinette stitch background. The contrast between the smooth knit stitches and the bumpy, dense, purl side of the reverse stockinette stitch allows the cable pattern to stand out clearly. Color and stitch patterns can also be incorporated for extra interest.

CABLE DICTIONARY:
Chapters one to six (pages 10–131)

With 100 stitches to inspire you, this cable dictionary covers everything from timeless classics to exciting, contemporary stitches.

The mix and match element enables you to tell at a glance how many repeats you would need to align two or more cables.

Skill-level indicator.

To save you time, we have included the stockinette equivalent calculation (SEC) for each stitch pattern so you can incorporate cables into your patterns.

Knitted examples show the individual stitches and the overall pattern.

Special stitches are explained on the page and can also be found in the glossary (pages 171–174).

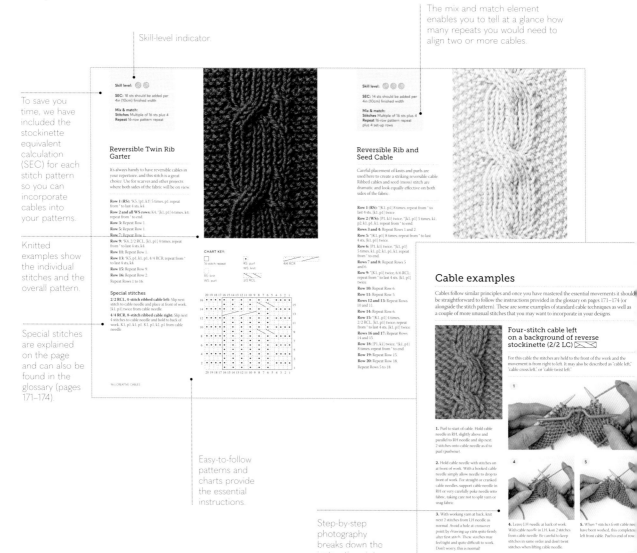

Easy-to-follow patterns and charts provide the essential instructions.

Step-by-step photography breaks down the instructions into clear parts.

CHAPTER SEVEN: CABLES: ESSENTIALS AND DESIGN

Whether you're new to cable knitting or wanting to learn how to use cables in your designs, this chapter will teach you all the key skills and techniques.

Cables follow similar principles, and once you have mastered the essential movements, it should be straightforward to follow the instructions provided. These are some examples of standard cable techniques as well as a couple of more unusual stitches.

Four-stitch cable right on a background of reverse stockinette (2/2 RC)

To create a cable that moves from left to right, the cable stitches are held to the back of the work. This technique may also be described as "cable right," "cable cross right," or "cable twist right."

...rd to start of cable. Hold cable ...le in RH, slightly above and ...lel to RH needle and slip next ...ches onto cable needle as if to ...(purlwise)

...ld cable needle with stitches on ...ck of work. With a hooked cable ...le simply allow needle to drop to ...of work. For straight or cranked ...needles, support cable needle in

RH or very carefully poke needle into fabric, taking care not to split yarn or snag fabric.

3. With working yarn at back, knit next 2 stitches from LH needle as normal. Avoid a hole at crossover point by drawing up yarn quite firmly after first stitch. These stitches may feel tight and quite difficult to work. Don't worry, this is normal!

4. Leave LH needle at back of work. With cable needle in LH, knit 2 stitches from cable needle. Be careful to keep stitches in same order and don't twist stitches when lifting cable needle

5. When 2 stitches from cable needle have been worked, this completes the right back cable. Purl to end of row.

Meet Debbie

I have been a passionate knitter since I was a child, learning from my granny when she came to visit from Scotland. As I got older, I learned much through trial and error (quite a lot of error!), before landing my first job knitting brightly colored mohair sweaters (thank you, 1980s).

At university, knitting took a back seat until I started work. After a busy day, I rediscovered the benefits and therapeutic relaxation of picking up a pair of needles, a ball of squishy yarn, and a cup of tea.

My first break as a professional designer came when one of my designs was spotted by a knitting magazine editor. Four years later, I was designing each issue as well as writing step-by-step tutorials. Three books later and I'm now working for another knitting magazine, writing the "agony aunt" column and the "how-to" features, answering questions from new and experienced knitters alike.

It is this experience that I hope to share in this, my fifth book. I want to give you all the skills you need to get started in cable knitting, master the essentials, and build your confidence to allow you to start your own knitting adventure.

CHAPTER ONE

Cable Classics

Here you will find all the essential cables that
are a mainstay of cable design. Timeless and
elegant enough to use on their own, or combine
with other cables to create new designs.

Skill level:

SEC: 2 sts should be added per 4in (10cm) finished width

Mix & match:
Stitches Multiple of 2 sts
Repeat 2-row pattern repeat

Two-stitch Cable— Short Left Twist

One of the simplest cables but a useful stitch for subtle accents. Can also be incorporated into a rib design.

Row 1 (RS): Knit.
Row 2 and all WS rows: Purl.
Row 3: 1/1 LC.
Row 4: Repeat Row 2.
Repeat Rows 3 and 4.

CHART KEY:

Set-up rows (work once only)

RS: knit
WS: purl

2-stitch repeat

1/1 LC

SEC: 2 sts should be added per 4in (10cm) finished width

Mix & match:
Stitches Multiple of 2 sts
Repeat 4-row pattern repeat

Two-stitch Cable—Medium Left Twist

By simply adding rows between the twists a softer cable is created that can be used as part of a panel or combination cable.

Row 1 (RS): Knit.
Row 2 and all WS rows: Purl.
Row 3: 1/1 LC.
Row 5: Repeat Row 1.
Row 6: Repeat Row 2.
Repeat Rows 3 to 6.

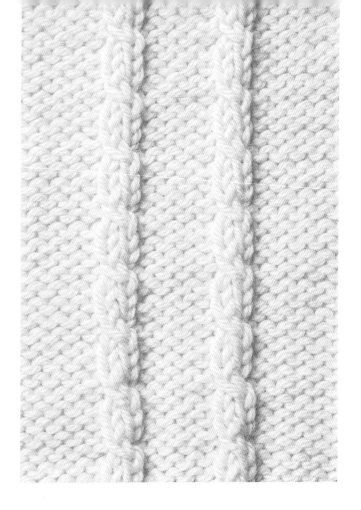

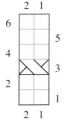

CHART KEY:

Set-up rows (work once only)

RS: knit
WS: purl

2-stitch repeat

1/1 LC

Skill level:

SEC: 2 sts should be added per 4in (10cm) finished width

Mix & match:
Stitches Multiple of 2 sts
Repeat 6-row pattern repeat

Two-stitch Cable— Long Left Twist

Extending the twists even farther apart gives an altogether different look. Narrow cables have many uses and it's possible to switch it up simply by changing the rows between the twists.

Row 1 (RS): Knit.
Row 2 and all WS rows: Purl.
Row 3: 1/1 LC
Row 5: Repeat Row 1.
Row 7: Repeat Row 1.
Row 8: Repeat Row 2.
Repeat Rows 3 to 8.

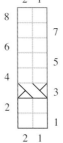

CHART KEY:

Set-up rows (work once only)

RS: knit
WS: purl

2-stitch repeat

1/1 LC

Skill level:

SEC: 2 sts should be added per 4in (10cm) finished width

Mix & match:
Stitches Multiple of 2 sts
Repeat 2-row pattern repeat

Two-stitch Cable— Short Right Twist

Taking the twist in the opposite direction gives a balanced pairing to the left twist. Place the two directly together or use them to "bookend" a panel for a great effect.

Row 1 (RS): Knit.
Row 2 and all WS rows: Purl.
Row 3: 1/1 RC.
Row 4: Repeat Row 2.
Repeat Rows 3 and 4.

CHART KEY:

☐ Set-up rows (work once only)

☐ RS: knit
WS: purl

☐ 2-stitch repeat

⧖ 1/1 RC

SEC: 2 sts should be added per 4in (10cm) finished width

Mix & match:
Stitches Multiple of 2 sts
Repeat 4-row pattern repeat

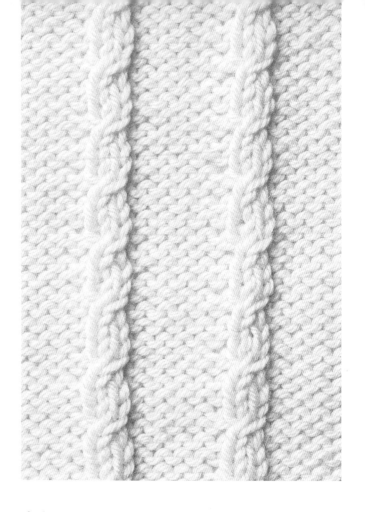

Two-stitch Cable— Medium Right Twist

Another pairing to mirror a left-twisting cable but can also be used to create an interesting all-over pattern.

Row 1 (RS): Knit.
Row 2 and all WS rows: Purl.
Row 3: 1/1 RC.
Row 5: Repeat Row 1.
Row 6: Repeat Row 2.
Repeat Rows 3 to 6.

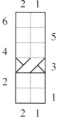

CHART KEY:

Set-up rows (work once only)

RS: knit
WS: purl

2-stitch repeat

1/1 RC

Skill level:

SEC: 2 sts should be added per 4in (10cm) finished width

Mix & match:
Stitches Multiple of 2 sts
Repeat 6-row pattern repeat

Two-stitch Cable— Long Right Twist

By experimenting with right and left twists and varying the length between twists, you can create a striking but stunning pattern just by using a simple two-stitch design.

Row 1 (RS): Knit.
Row 2 and all WS rows: Purl.
Row 3: 1/1 RC.
Row 5: Repeat Row 1.
Row 7: Repeat Row 1.
Row 8: Repeat Row 2.
Repeat Rows 3 to 8.

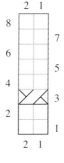

CHART KEY:

Set-up rows (work once only)

RS: knit
WS: purl

2-stitch repeat

1/1 RC

Skill level:

SEC: 11 sts should be added per 4in (10cm) finished width

Mix & match:
Stitches Multiple of 4 sts
Repeat 2-row pattern repeat

Four-stitch Cable— Short Left Twist

A very popular cable both on its own or combined with other cables as part of a panel. Stylish but straightforward to work.

Row 1 (RS): Knit.
Row 2 and all WS rows: Purl.
Row 3: 2/2 LC.
Row 4: Repeat Row 2.
Repeat Rows 3 and 4.

CHART KEY:

Set-up rows (work once only)

RS: knit
WS: purl

4-stitch repeat

2/2 LC

Skill level: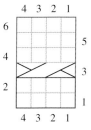

SEC: 2 sts should be added per 4in (10cm) finished width

Mix & match:
Stitches Multiple of 4 sts
Repeat 4-row pattern repeat

Four-stitch Cable—Medium Right Twist

Four-stitch cables are striking enough to be used on their own, for example along a sleeve or as a single or multiple panel. They are easy to work and add texture without distorting the fabric.

Row 1 (RS): Knit.
Row 2 and all WS rows: Purl.
Row 3: 2/2 RC.
Row 5: Repeat Row 1.
Row 6: Repeat Row 2.
Repeat Rows 3 to 6.

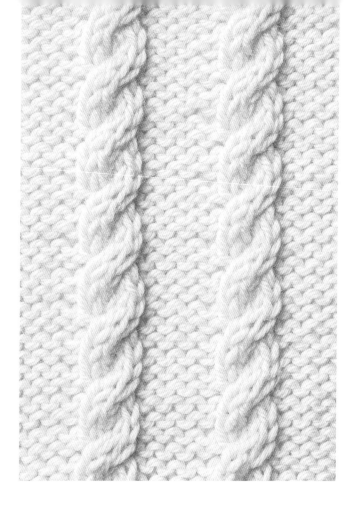

CHART KEY:

☐ Set-up rows (work once only)

☐ RS: knit
WS: purl

☐ 4-stitch repeat

⧖ 2/2 RC

SEC: 13 sts should be added per 4in (10cm) finished width

Mix & match:
Stitches Multiple of 8 sts
Repeat 4-row pattern repeat

Eight-stitch Cable— Medium Left Twist

Wider cables are a little trickier to work as they require holding more stitches on the cable needle. However, they do give dramatic effects.

Row 1 (RS): Knit.
Row 2 and all WS rows: Purl.
Row 3: 4/4 LC.
Row 5: Repeat Row 1.
Row 6: Repeat Row 2.
Repeat Rows 3 to 6.

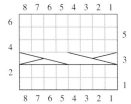

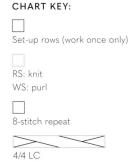

CHART KEY:

Set-up rows (work once only)

RS: knit
WS: purl

8-stitch repeat

4/4 LC

Skill level:

SEC: 9 sts should be added per 4in (10cm) finished width

Mix & match:
Stitches Multiple of 8 sts
Repeat 6-row pattern repeat

Eight-stitch Cable— Long Right Twist

With wider cables, increasing the rows between the twists can make them easier to work. They are also less likely to distort the surrounding fabric.

Row 1 (RS): Knit.
Row 2 and all WS rows: Purl.
Row 3: 4/4 RC.
Row 5: Repeat Row 1.
Row 7: Repeat Row 1.
Row 8: Repeat Row 2.
Repeat Rows 3 to 8.

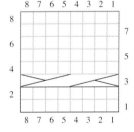

CHART KEY:

Set-up rows (work once only)

RS: knit
WS: purl

8-stitch repeat

4/4 RC

Skill level:

SEC: 11 sts should be added per 4in (10cm) finished width

Mix & match:
Stitches Multiple of 12 sts
Repeat 14-row pattern repeat

Twelve-stitch Cable— Long Left Twist

As cables get wider, be sure to make a large swatch when testing gauge. Wide cables make lovely centerpieces but can also be effectively combined in a panel.

Row 1 (RS): Knit.
Row 2 and all WS rows: Purl.
Row 3: Repeat Row 1.
Row 5: 6/6 LC.
Row 7: Repeat Row 1.
Row 9: Repeat Row 1.
Row 11: Repeat Row 1.
Row 13: Repeat Row 1.
Row 15: Repeat Row 1.
Row 17: Repeat Row 1.
Row 18: Repeat Row 2.
Repeat Rows 5 to 18.

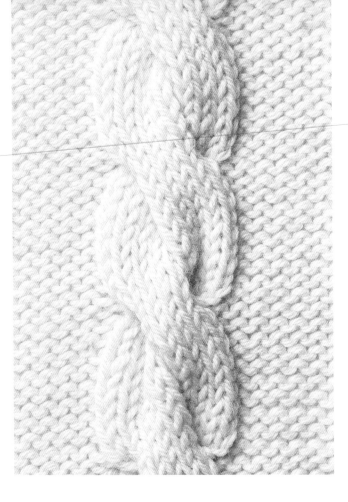

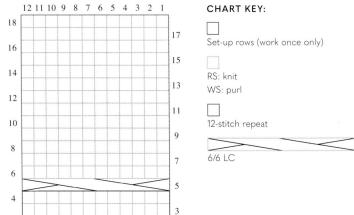

CHART KEY:

Set-up rows (work once only)

RS: knit
WS: purl

12-stitch repeat

6/6 LC

Skill level:

SEC: 6 sts should be added per 4in (10cm) finished width

Mix & match:
Stitches Multiple of 12 sts
Repeat 16-row pattern repeat

Twelve-stitch Cable— Extra Long Right Twist

When making wide cables with lots of rows between the twists, plan carefully to ensure that the end of the repeat falls as you would like. Pairing with a narrow, short repeat twist can look particularly effective.

Row 1 (RS): Knit.
Row 2 and all WS rows: Purl.
Row 3: Repeat Row 1.
Row 5: 6/6 RC.
Row 7: Repeat Row 1.
Row 9: Repeat Row 1.
Row 11: Repeat Row 1.
Row 13: Repeat Row 1.
Row 15: Repeat Row 1.
Row 17: Repeat Row 1.
Row 19: Repeat Row 1.
Row 20: Repeat Row 2.
Repeat Rows 5 to 20.

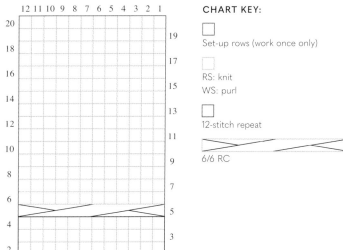

CHART KEY:

Set-up rows (work once only)

RS: knit
WS: purl

12-stitch repeat

6/6 RC

Twelve-stitch Descending Cable— Left Twist

This interesting stitch uses different width cables to create an unusual pyramid shape. It would look great used instead of a rib on a soft cuff or edging.

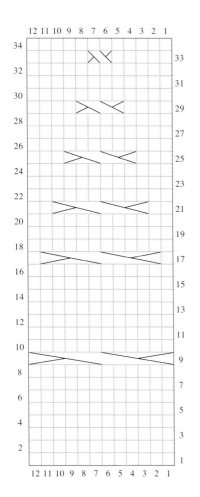

Row 1 (RS): Knit.

Row 2 and all WS rows: Purl.

Row 3: Repeat Row 1.

Row 5: Repeat Row 1.

Row 7: Repeat Row 1.

Row 9: 6/6 LC.

Row 11: Repeat Row 1.

Row 13: Repeat Row 1.

Row 15: Repeat Row 1.

Row 17: K1, 5/5 LC, k1.

Row 19: Repeat Row 1.

Row 21: K2, 4/4 LC, k2.

Row 23: Repeat Row 1.

Row 25: K3, 3/3 LC, k3.

Row 27: Repeat Row 1.

Row 29: K4, 2/2 LC, k4.

Row 31: Repeat Row 1.

Row 33: K5, 1/1 LC, k5.

Row 34: Repeat Row 2.

Repeat Rows 1 to 34.

CHART KEY:

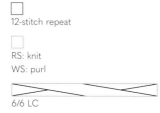

12-stitch repeat

RS: knit
WS: purl

6/6 LC

5/5 LC

4/4 LC

3/3 LC

2/2 LC

1/1 LC

SEC: 0 sts should be added per 4in (10cm) finished width

Mix & match:
Stitches Multiple of 12 sts
Repeat 14-row pattern repeat

Twelve-stitch Asymmetric Purl Cable— Left Twist

Cables don't need to be symmetrical, and incorporating some purl stitches can add even more interest.

Row 1 (RS): Knit.
Row 2 (WS): Purl.
Rows 3 to 10: Repeat Rows 1 and 2.
Row 11: 4/8 LPC.
Row 12: P4, k8.
Row 13: P8, k4.
Rows 14 to 24: Repeat Rows 12 and 13.
Repeat Rows 11 to 24.

Special stitch

4/8 LPC: Slip next 4 stitches to cable needle and place at front of work. Purl next 8 stitches, then k4 from cable needle.

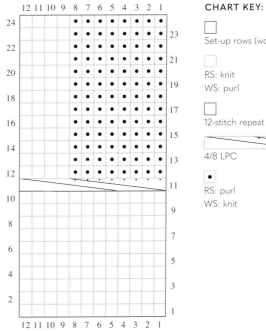

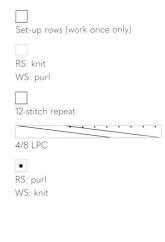

CHART KEY:

Set-up rows (work once only)

RS: knit
WS: purl

12-stitch repeat

4/8 LPC

•
RS: purl
WS: knit

Fifteen-stitch Ascending Cable— Right Twist

Inverting the cables from the twelve-stitch Descending Cable on page 24 and giving them a right twist creates a different effect that would look great around the yoke of a top-down sweater.

Skill level:

SEC: 0 sts should be added per 4in (10cm) finished width

Mix & match:
Stitches Multiple of 15 sts plus 1
Repeat 36-row pattern repeat

Row 1 (RS): *P7, k2, p6; repeat from * to last st, p1.

Row 2 (WS): K1, *k6, p2, k7; repeat from * to end.

Rows 3 to 8: Repeat Rows 1 and 2.

Row 9: *P6, k1, 1/1 RC, k1, p5; repeat from * to last st, p1.

Row 10: K1, *k5, p4, k6 ; repeat from * to end.

Row 11: *P6, k4, p5 ; repeat from * to last st, p1.

Row 12: Repeat Row 10.

Row 13: *P5, k1, 2/2 RC, k1, p4; repeat from * to last st, p1.

Row 14: K1, *k4, p6, k5; repeat from * to end.

Row 15: *P5, k6, p4; repeat from * to last st, p1.

Row 16: Repeat Row 14.

Row 17: *P4, k1, 3/3 RC, k1, p3; repeat from * to last st, p1.

Row 18: K1, *k3, p8, k4; repeat from * to end.

Row 19: *P4, k8, p3 ; repeat from * to last st, p1.

Row 20: Repeat Row 18.

Row 21: *P3, k1, 4/4 RC, k1, p2 ; repeat from * to last st, p1.

Row 22: K1, *k2, p10, k3 ; repeat from * to end.

Row 23: *P3, k10, p2; repeat from * to last st, p1.

Row 24: Repeat Row 22.

Row 25: *P2, k1, 5/5 RC, k1, p1; repeat from * to last st, p1.

Row 26: K1, *k1, p12, k2; repeat from * to end.

Row 27: *P2, k12, p1; repeat from * to last st, p1.

Row 28: Repeat Row 26.

Row 29: *P1, k1, 6/6 RC, k1; repeat from * to last st, p1.

Row 30: K1, *p14, k1; repeat from * to end.

Row 31: *P1, k14 ; repeat from * to last st, p1.

Rows 32 to 35: Repeat Rows 30 and 31.

Row 36: Repeat Row 30.

Repeat Rows 1 to 36.

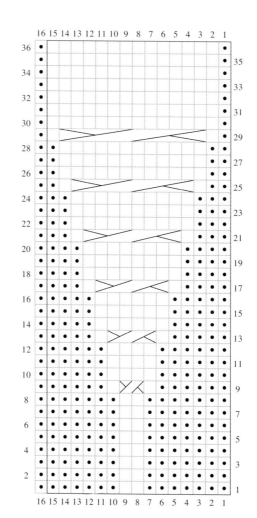

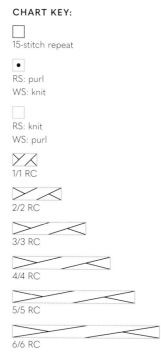

CHART KEY:

15-stitch repeat

RS: purl
WS: knit

RS: knit
WS: purl

1/1 RC

2/2 RC

3/3 RC

4/4 RC

5/5 RC

6/6 RC

SEC: 8 sts should be added per 4in (10cm) finished width

Mix & match:
Stitches Multiple of 12 sts
Repeat 12-row pattern repeat

Nine-stitch Double Twist Cable—Right Twist

A more intricate cable but there are only two rows with twists so this is not as complex as it looks!

Row 1 (RS): Knit.

Row 2 and all WS rows: Purl.

Row 3: Repeat Row 1.

Row 5: Repeat Row 1.

Row 7: Repeat Row 1.

Row 9: K3, 3/6 RC.

Row 11: 3/6 RC, k3.

Row 12: Repeat Row 2.

Repeat Rows 1 to 12.

Special stitch

3/6 RC: Slip next 6 stitches to cable needle and hold to back of work. K next 3 stitches from LH needle. K6 from cable needle.

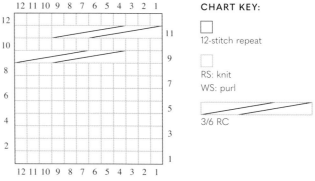

CHART KEY:

12-stitch repeat

RS: knit
WS: purl

3/6 RC

Skill level:

SEC: 11 sts should be added per 4in (10cm) finished width

Mix & match:
Stitches Multiple of 8 sts
Repeat 16-row pattern repeat

Eight-stitch Simple Wiggle Cable

A four-stitch cable weaves, serpentlike, over the remaining four stitches, rather than taking the more usual under-and-over route. This creates a charming, textured surface that can be combined with a range of other stitches.

Row 1 (RS): Knit.
Row 2 and all WS rows: Purl.
Row 3: Repeat Row 1.
Row 5: Repeat Row 1.
Row 7: 4/4 LC.
Row 9: Repeat Row 1.
Row 11: Repeat Row 1.
Row 13: Repeat Row 1.
Row 15: 4/4 RC.
Row 16: Repeat Row 2.
Repeat Rows 1 to 16.

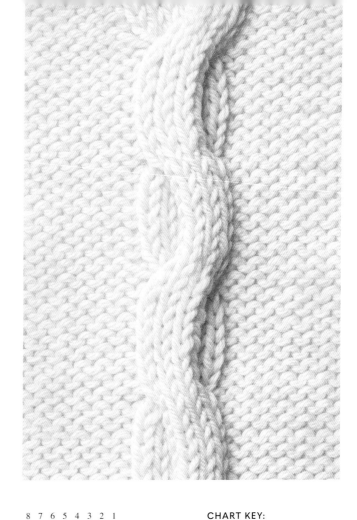

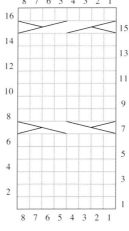

CHART KEY:

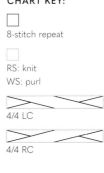

8-stitch repeat

RS: knit
WS: purl

4/4 LC

4/4 RC

Ten-stitch Threaded Figure-eight Cable

A single cable winds its way through two figure-eight twists to create a richly textured, detailed stitch.

Skill level:

SEC: 8 sts should be added per 4in (10cm) finished width

Mix & match:
Stitches Multiple of 10 sts
Repeat 32-row pattern repeat

Row 1 (RS): Knit.
Row 2 and all WS rows: Purl.
Row 3: Knit.
Row 5: Repeat Row 3.
Row 7: 5/5 RC.
Row 9: Repeat Row 3.
Row 11: Repeat Row 3.
Row 13: 3/2 LC, 3/2 RC.

Row 15: Repeat Row 3.
Row 17: 3/2 RC, 3/2 LC.
Row 19: Repeat Row 3.
Row 21: Repeat Row 3.
Row 23: 5/5 LC.
Row 25: Repeat Row 3.
Row 27: Repeat Row 3.
Row 29: Repeat Row 13.

Row 31: Repeat Row 3.
Row 33: Repeat Row 17.
Row 34: Repeat Row 2.
Repeat Rows 3 to 34.

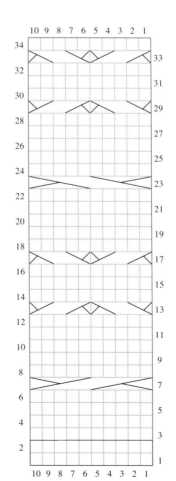

CHART KEY:

☐ Set-up rows (work once only)

☐ RS: knit
WS: purl

☐ 10-stitch repeat

5/5 RC

3/2 LC

3/2 RC

5/5 LC

CHAPTER TWO

Cable Combinations

In this chapter we take our classic cables and combine them in interesting ways to produce new designs. Cables may be simply arranged together, mirrored, or wrapped for exciting new effects. We also bring in new stitches and infills to extend your design repertoire.

Skill level:

SEC: 8 sts should be added per 4in (10cm) finished width

Mix & match:
Stitches Multiple of 13 sts
Repeat 4-row pattern repeat

Tire Tracks

This complex-looking stitch actually only has one row of cables, yet it looks rich and densely textured. It would make a great feature panel or could be combined within a larger panel.

Row 1 (RS): Knit.
Row 2 and all WS rows: Purl.
Row 3: 3/3 LC, k1, 3/3 RC.
Row 5: Repeat Row 1.
Row 6: Repeat Row 2.
Repeat Rows 3 to 6.

CHART KEY:

Set-up rows
(work once only)

13-stitch repeat

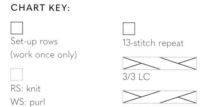
3/3 LC

RS: knit
WS: purl

3/3 RC

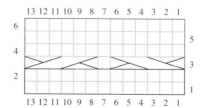

13 12 11 10 9 8 7 6 5 4 3 2 1

13 12 11 10 9 8 7 6 5 4 3 2 1

Skill level: ◐ ◐ ◐

SEC: 5 sts should be added per 4in (10cm) finished width

Mix & match:
Stitches Multiple of 15 sts
Repeat 4-row pattern repeat

Lace and Cable Panel

This panel is a combination of two-stitch cables and a central lace section. It would be ideal as a single, central panel but could also form an interesting repeated panel on a sweater, or be lovely as an edging for a jacket.

Row 1 (RS): K4, p1, k5, p1, k4.
Row 2 and all WS rows: P4, k1, p5, k1, p4.
Row 3: 1/1 RC, 1/1 LC, p1, k1, yo, cdd, yo, k1, p1, 1/1 RC, 1/1 LC.
Row 5: 1/1 RC, k2, p1, k1, yo, cdd, yo, k1, p1, k2, 1/1 LC.
Repeat Rows 2 to 5.

Special stitch

cdd, central double decrease: Slip 2 stitches together, k1, then pass slipped stitches over.

CHART KEY:

□ Set-up rows (work once only)	▪ RS: purl / WS: knit	⧅ 1/1 LC
□ RS: knit / WS: purl	□ 15-stitch repeat	○ yo
	⧄ 1/1 RC	⋀ cdd

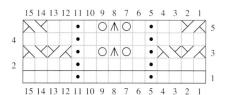

Skill level:

SEC: 15 sts should be added per 4in (10cm) finished width

Mix & match:
Stitches Multiple of 15 sts
Repeat 4-row pattern repeat

Rapunzel Braid

This intricate braid looks complicated to make but is simply the careful placement of two cable rows. It does form a dense fabric so care is needed when swatched as a panel. It would be great as a jacket edging where a firmer fabric is needed.

Row 1 (RS): Knit.
Row 2 and all WS rows: Purl.
Row 3: K3, [3/3 LC] twice.
Row 5: [3/3 RC] twice, k3.
Row 6: Repeat Row 2.
Repeat Rows 3 to 6.

CHART KEY:

☐ Set-up rows (work once only)

☐ RS: knit WS: purl

☐ . 15-stitch repeat

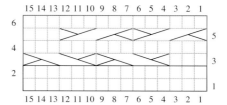

3/3 RC

3/3 LC

Skill level: ⊕ ⊕ ⊕

SEC: 7 sts should be added per 4in (10cm) finished width

Mix & match:
Stitches Multiple of 9 sts
Repeat 8-row pattern repeat

Three-cable Braid

Although this braid is richly textured it produces a soft fabric that could be worked as a single panel, perhaps down a sleeve or garment front. Several braids could be worked side by side or as part of a larger panel.

Row 1 (RS): Knit.
Row 2 (WS): Purl.
Row 3: 2/1 LPC, 2/1 RPC, 2/1 LPC.
Row 4: P2, k2, p4, k1.
Row 5: P1, 2/2 RC, p2, k2.
Row 6: Repeat Row 4.
Row 7: 2/1 RPC, 2/1 LPC, 2/1 RPC.
Row 8: K1, p4, k2, p2.
Row 9: K2, p2, 2/2 LC, p1.
Row 10: Repeat Row 8.
Repeat Rows 3 to 10.

CHART KEY:

☐
Set-up rows
(work once only)

☐
RS: knit
WS: purl

☐
9-stitch repeat

⧄ 2/1 LPC

⧄ 2/1 RPC

▪
RS: purl
WS: knit

⧄ 2/2 RC

⧄ 2/2 LC

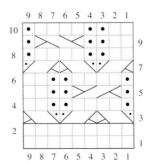

Wrapped Hourglass Cable

Two rows of simple wrapped stitches create added interest to this otherwise straightforward cable. The cable stitches use both knit and purl stitches, which require a little more care when working. This allows the uninterrupted flow of the cable design against the purl background.

Skill level:

SEC: 6 sts should be added per 4in (10cm) finished width

Mix & match:
Stitches Multiple of 8 sts
Repeat 10-row pattern repeat

Row 1 (RS): P2, k4, p2.
Row 2 (WS): K2, p4, k2.
Row 3: P1, 2/1 RPC, 2/1 LPC, p1.
Row 4: K1, p2, k2, p2, k1.
Row 5: 2/1 RPC, p2, 2/1 LPC.
Row 6: P2, k4, p2.
Row 7: 2/1 LPC, p2, 2/1 RPC.

Row 8: Repeat Row 4.
Row 9: P1, 2/1 LPC, 2/1 RPC, p1.
Row 10: Repeat Row 2.
Row 11: P2, wrap 4 sts, p2.
Row 12: K2, wrap 4 sts, k2.
Repeat Rows 3 to 12.

Special stitches

wrap 4 sts: RS slip 4 stitches with yarn at back, pass yarn to front, slip the 4 stitches back to the left needle, k4.

wrap 4 sts: WS slip 4 stitches with yarn at back, pass yarn to front, slip the 4 stitches back to the left needle, p4.

CHART KEY:

Set-up rows
(work once only)

• RS: purl
WS: knit

RS: knit
WS: purl

8-stitch repeat

2/1 RPC

2/1 LPC

 wrap 4 sts

Skill level:

SEC: 4 sts should be added per 4in (10cm) finished width

Mix & match:
Stitches Multiple of 12 sts
Repeat 8-row pattern repeat

Vertebrae

It's hard to believe this beautifully textured stitch has just a single cable row. It produces a deeply textured fabric and would normally be used as a single panel but with careful attention to swatching, an all-over pattern could be achieved.

Row 1 (RS): Knit.
Row 2 (WS): Purl.
Row 3: Repeat Row 1.
Row 4: Repeat Row 2.
Row 5: Repeat Row 1.
Row 6: Repeat Row 2.
Row 7: 3/3 RC, 3/3 LC.
Row 8: Repeat Row 2.
Repeat Rows 1 to 8.

CHART KEY:

12-stitch repeat

RS: knit
WS: purl

3/3 RC

3/3 LC

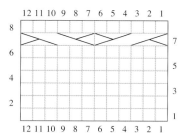

Twelve-stitch Inverted Vertebrae

Compare this stitch to the Vertebrae opposite, and you will see that it is only the arrangement of the two cables that has been changed. To invert the cable, work the left (front) cable first, then the right (back) cable. These two stitches work well together to create an interesting all-over pattern.

Row 1 (RS): Knit.
Row 2 (WS): Purl.
Row 3: Repeat Row 1.
Row 4: Repeat Row 2.
Row 5: Repeat Row 1.
Row 6: Repeat Row 2.
Row 7: 3/3 LC, 3/3 RC.
Row 8: Repeat Row 2.
Repeat Rows 1 to 8.

CHART KEY:

☐ 12-stitch repeat

☐ RS: knit
WS: purl

3/3 LC

3/3 RC

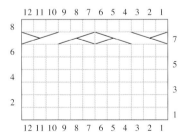

Skill level:

SEC: 11 sts should be added per 4in (10cm) finished width

Mix & match:
Stitches Multiple of 22 sts
Repeat 10-row pattern repeat

Sixteen-stitch Wishbone Rib Cable

Choose your favorite with this cable as it looks equally stunning from both sides. Although it takes a little concentration to make sure that the ribs and cables stay aligned, there is just one cable row.

Row 1 (RS): P1, k2, p1, [k2, p2] 3 times, k2, p1, k2, p1.
Row 2 (WS): K1, p2, k1, [p2, k2] 3 times, p2, k1, p2, k1.
Row 3: Repeat Row 1.
Row 4: Repeat Row 2.
Row 5: Repeat Row 1.
Row 6: Repeat Row 2.
Row 7: Repeat Row 1.
Row 8: Repeat Row 2.
Row 9: K1, p2, [1/2/1 RC, 1/2/1 LC] twice, p2, k1.
Row 10: Repeat Row 2.
Repeat Rows 1 to 10.

Special stitches

1/2/1 RC: Slip next 4 stitches to cable needle and place at back of work, [p1, k2, p1] then p1, k2, p1 from cable needle.

1/2/1 LC: Slip next 4 stitches to cable needle and place at front of work, [p1, k2, p1] then p1, k2, p1 from cable needle.

CHART KEY:

22-stitch repeat

1/2/1 RC

•
RS: purl
WS: knit

1/2/1 LC

RS: knit
WS: purl

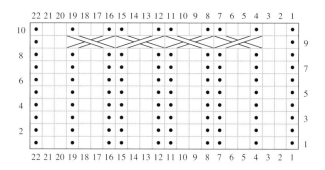

Skill level: ◉ ◉ ◉

SEC: 6 sts should be added per 4in (10cm) finished width

Mix & match:
Stitches Multiple of 22 sts
Repeat 10-row pattern repeat

Sixteen-stitch Hourglass Rib Cable

This is another fascinating stitch that looks equally beautiful on both sides due to the ribbed fabric. One side (with the reverse stockinette background) is a little softer, the knit side is deeper, and the ribs more visible. It could be used very effectively to "grow" out of a 2 x 2 ribbed edge or cuff.

Row 1 (RS): P1, k2, p1, [k2, p2] 3 times, k2, p1, k2, p1.
Row 2 and all WS rows: K1, p2, k1, [p2, k2] 3 times, p2, k1, p2, k1.
Row 3: Repeat Row 1.
Row 5: P1, k2, [1/2/1 RC, 1/2/1 LC] twice, k2, p1.
Row 7: Repeat Row 1.
Row 9: P1, k2, [1/2/1 LC, 1/2/1 RC] twice, k2, p1.
Row 10: Repeat Row 2.
Repeat Rows 1 to 10.

Special stitches

1/2/1 RC: Slip next 4 stitches to cable needle and place at back of work, [p1, k2, p1] then p1, k2, p1 from cable needle.

1/2/1 LC: Slip next 4 stitches to cable needle and place at front of work, [p1, k2, p1] then p1, k2, p1 from cable needle.

CHART KEY:

☐ 22-stitch repeat

 1/2/1 RC

• RS: purl
WS: knit

 1/2/1 LC

☐ RS: knit
WS: purl

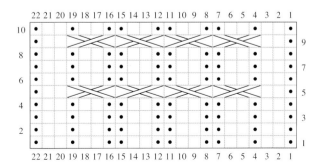

Skill level:

SEC: 6 sts should be added per 4in (10cm) finished width

Mix & match:
Stitches Multiple of 6 sts
Repeat 10-row pattern repeat

Linked Cable

A neat, tidy stitch that can be used singly or combined as part of a larger panel. The cable row is a little tricky as it involves moving the cable twice and incorporating both knit and purl stitches.

Row 1 (RS): k2, p2, k2.
Row 2 (WS): P2, k2, p2.
Row 3: Repeat Row 1.
Row 4: Repeat Row 2.
Row 5: 2/2/2 RPC.
Row 6: Repeat Row 2.
Row 7: Repeat Row 1.
Rows 8: Repeat Row 2.
Row 9: Repeat Row 1.
Row 10: Repeat Row 2.
Row 11: Repeat Row 1.
Row 12: Repeat Row 2.
Repeat Rows 3 to 12.

Special stitch

2/2/2 RPC: Slip next 4 stitches to cable needle and place at front of work, k2, slip 2 left-most stitches from cable needle to LH needle, move the cable needle with remaining stitches to back of work, p2 from the LH needle, then k2 from cable needle.

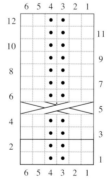

CHART KEY:

☐ Set-up rows (work once only)

☐ RS: knit
WS: purl

• RS: purl
WS: knit

☐ 6-stitch repeat

⤬ 2/2/2 RPC

Skill level:

SEC: 4 sts should be added per 4in (10cm) finished width

Mix & match:
Stitches Multiple of 13 sts
Repeat 16-row pattern repeat

Hourglass

This bold stitch has a lovely soft, flowing feel. Spacing out the cable rows (and there are only two per repeat) gives a really open, sumptuous effect. Use this stitch alone as a centerpiece or perhaps pair two with a honeycomb or lattice in-between to form a beautiful framed panel.

Row 1 (RS): Knit.
Row 2 and all WS rows: Purl.
Row 3: Repeat Row 1.
Row 5: 3/3 LC, k1, 3/3 RC.
Row 7: Repeat Row 1.
Row 9: Repeat Row 1.
Row 11: Repeat Row 1.
Row 13: 3/3 RC, k1, 3/3 LC.
Row 15: Repeat Row 1.
Row 16: Repeat Row 2.
Repeat Rows 1 to 16.

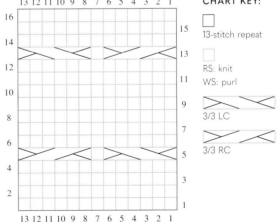

CHART KEY:

13-stitch repeat

RS: knit
WS: purl

3/3 LC

3/3 RC

SEC: 6 sts should be added per 4in (10cm) finished width

Mix & match:
Stitches Multiple of 22 sts
Repeat 8-row pattern repeat

Staghorn Cable

This is a broad cable with a 22-stitch repeat. It would make a striking pattern used alone or could be combined with narrow braids or cables to produce a very effective large panel.

Row 1 (RS): Knit.
Row 2 (WS): Purl.
Rows 3 and 4: Repeat Rows 1 and 2.
Row 5: K6, 3/2 RC, 3/2 LC, k6.
Row 6: Repeat Row 2.
Row 7: K4, 3/2 RC, k4, 3/2 LC, k4.
Row 8: Repeat Row 2.
Row 9: K2, 3/2 RC, k8, 3/2 LC, k2.
Row 10: Repeat Row 2.
Row 11: 3/2 RC, k12, 3/2 LC.
Row 12: Repeat Row 2.
Repeat Rows 5 to 12.

CHART KEY:

Set-up rows (work once only)

RS: knit
WS: purl

22-stitch repeat

3/2 RC

3/2 LC

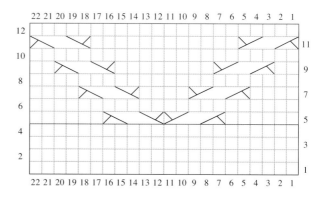

SEC: 0 sts should be added per 4in (10cm) finished width

Mix & match:
Stitches Multiple of 8 sts
Repeat 20-row pattern repeat

Intersected Cable and Stockinette

This narrow cable has just one cable but filling the center with a ladder of stockinette and garter stitch adds interest. You could vary this by filling entirely with garter stitch or by adjusting the length between the repeats if you are incorporating this into a panel with other stitches.

Row 1 (RS): Knit.
Row 2 (WS): Purl.
Row 3: Repeat Row 1.
Row 4: Repeat Row 2.
Row 5: 4/4 LC.
Row 6: Repeat Row 2.
Row 7: Repeat Row 1.
Row 8: Repeat Row 2.
Row 9: Repeat Row 1.
Row 10: P2, k4, p2.
Row 11: K2, p4, k2.
Row 12: Repeat Row 10.
Row 13: Repeat Row 1.
Rows 14 to 20: Repeat Rows 6 to 12.

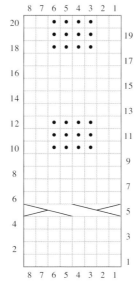

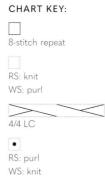

CHART KEY:

8-stitch repeat

RS: knit
WS: purl

4/4 LC

RS: purl
WS: knit

Twisted Heart

This is a complex stitch as it incorporates a range of standard cables and knit/purl cables. However, the effect is great and makes a super centerpiece to a design.

Skill level:

SEC: 7 sts should be added per 4in (10cm) finished width

Mix & match:
Stitches Multiple of 24 sts
Repeat 20-row pattern repeat

Row 1 (RS): P9, k6, p9.

Row 2 (WS): K9, p6, k9.

Row 3: Repeat Row 1.

Row 4: Repeat Row 2.

Row 5: Repeat Row 1.

Row 6: Repeat Row 2.

Row 7: P9, 3/3 RC, p9.

Row 8: Repeat Row 2.

Row 9: P6, 3/3 RC, 3/3 LC, p6.

Row 10: K6, p12, k6.

Row 11: P3, 3/3 RPC, k6, 3/3 LPC, p3.

Row 12: K3, p3, k3, p6, k3, p3, k3.

Row 13: P1, 3/2 RPC, p3, 3/3 RC, p3, 3/2 LPC, p1.

Row 14: K1, p3, k5, p6, k5, p3, k1.

Row 15: 3/1 RPC, p5, k6, p5, 3/1 LPC.

Row 16: P3, k6, p6, k6, p3.

Row 17: K3, p6, 3/3 RC, p6, k3.

Row 18: Repeat Row 16.

Row 19: 3/3 LPC, 3/3 RC, 3/3 LC, 3/3 RPC.

Row 20: Repeat Row 2.

Repeat Rows 1 to 20.

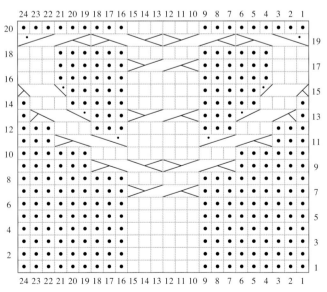

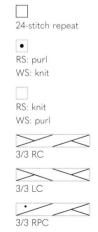

CHART KEY:

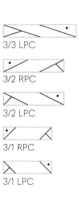

24-stitch repeat

•
RS: purl
WS: knit

RS: knit
WS: purl

3/3 RC

3/3 LC

3/3 RPC

3/3 LPC

3/2 RPC

3/2 LPC

3/1 RPC

3/1 LPC

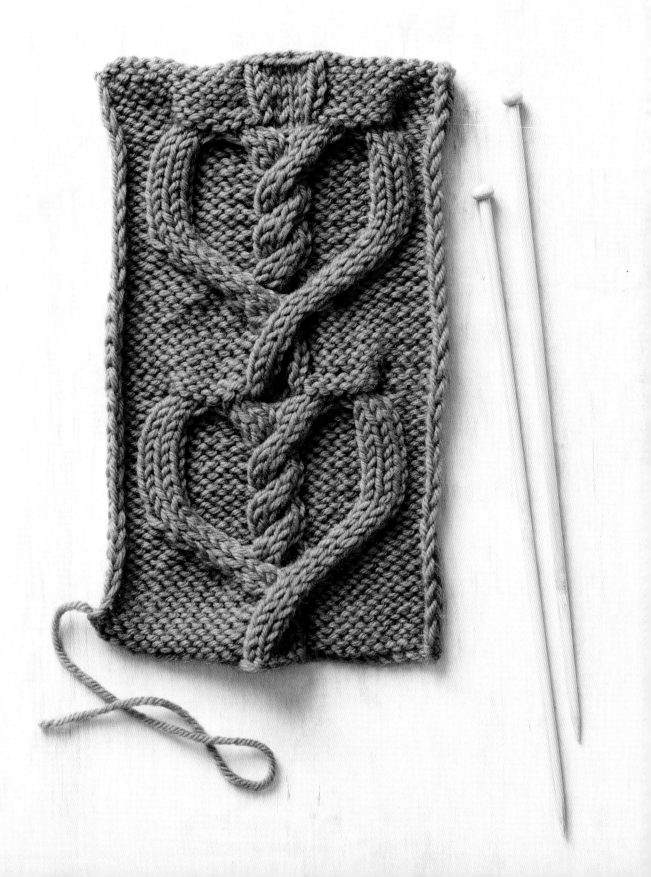

Skill level: ◔ ◔

SEC: 4 sts should be added per 4in (10cm) finished width

Mix & match:
Stitches Multiple of 12 sts
Repeat 28-row pattern repeat

Garter Wrapped Rib Cable

Just two cable stitches are required for this richly textured, dense cable. A little care is needed with the garter and rib stitches to keep the patterns aligned.

Row 1 (RS): [K1, p1] twice, k4, [p1, k1] twice.
Row 2 and all WS rows: P1, k1, p1, k6, p1, k1, p1.
Row 3: Repeat Row 1.
Row 5: [K1, p1] twice, 4/4 LC.
Row 7: 4/4 RC, [p1, k1] twice.
Row 9: Repeat Row 1.
Row 11: Repeat Row 1.
Row 13: Repeat Row 1.
Row 15: Repeat Row 1.
Row 17: Repeat Row 1.
Row 19: 4/4 LC, [p1, k1] twice.
Row 21: [K1, p1] twice, 4/4 RC.
Row 23: Repeat Row 1.
Row 25: Repeat Row 1.
Row 27: Repeat Row 1.
Row 28: Repeat Row 2.
Repeat Rows 1 to 28.

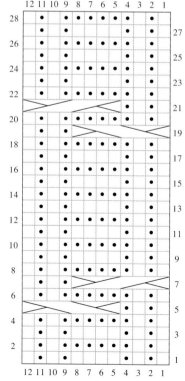

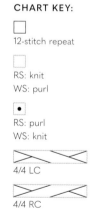

CHART KEY:

☐ 12-stitch repeat

☐ RS: knit
WS: purl

• RS: purl
WS: knit

4/4 LC

4/4 RC

Skill level:

SEC: 4 sts should be added per 4in (10cm) finished width

Mix & match:
Stitches Multiple of 13 sts
Repeat 4-row pattern repeat

Mirrored Twining Cable

This striking pattern is created using just a pair of 2-stitch cables, one slanting left and one right. You could play with single panels of this stitch or rearrange the left and right slants to create a wide variety of new designs.

Row 1 (RS): [1/1 RC] 3 times, p1, [1/1 LC] 3 times.
Row 2 (WS): P6, k1, p6.
Row 3: K1, [1/1 RC] twice, k1, p1, k1, [1/1 LC] twice, k1.
Row 4: Repeat Row 2.
Repeat Rows 1 to 4.

CHART KEY:

☐ 13-stitch repeat

▱ ▱ 1/1 RC

• RS: purl WS: knit

▱ ▱ 1/1 LC

☐ RS: knit WS: purl

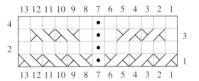

Skill level:

SEC: 2 sts should be added per 4in (10cm) finished width

Mix & match:
Stitches Multiple of 13 sts
Repeat 16-row pattern repeat

Seed-filled Lattice

This straightforward lattice is enhanced with a center of seed stitch, giving it an interesting twist. It could be used as a single panel or combined to produce an all-over design.

Row 1 (RS): P4, k5, p4.
Row 2 (WS): K4, p5, k4.
Row 3: P3, 2/1 RC, p1, 2/1 LC, p3.
Row 4: K3, p2, k1, p1, k1, p2, k3.
Row 5: P2, 2/1 RPC, k1, p1, k1, 2/1 LPC, p2.
Row 6: K2, p3, k1, p1, k1, p3, k2.
Row 7: P1, 2/1 RC, [p1, k1] twice, p1, 2/1 LC, p1.
Row 8: K1, p2, [k1, p1] 3 times, k1, p2, k1.
Row 9: 2/1 RPC, [k1, p1] 3 times, k1, 2/1 LPC.
Row 10: P3, [k1, p1] 3 times, k1, p3.
Row 11: 2/1 LC, [k1, p1] 3 times, k1, 2/1 RC.
Row 12: Repeat Row 8.
Row 13: P1, 2/1 LC, [p1, k1] twice, p1, 2/1 RC, p1.
Row 14: Repeat Row 6.
Row 15: P2, 2/1 LC, k1, p1, k1, 2/1 RC, p2.
Row 16: Repeat Row 4.
Row 17: P3, 2/1 LC, p1, 2/1 RC, p3.
Row 18: K4, p5, k4.
Repeat Rows 3 to 18.

CHART KEY:

☐ Set-up rows (work once only)

• RS: purl WS: knit

☐ RS: knit WS: purl

☐ 13-stitch repeat

2/1 RC

2/1 LC

2/1 RPC

2/1 LPC

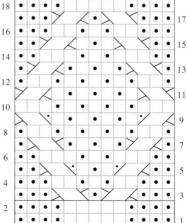

Skill level:

SEC: 10 sts should be added per 4in (10cm) finished width

Mix & match:
Stitches Multiple of 16 sts
Repeat 18-row pattern repeat

Seaweed

There's a lot going on with this advanced cable, but it does create a beautiful, softly twining effect like leaves or waving seaweed. A single repeat would look very effective as the lower edge to a sweater or jacket.

Row 1 (RS): Knit.
Row 2 (WS): Purl.
Row 3: P6, k6, p4.
Row 4: K4, p6, k6.
Row 5: P3, 3/3 RPC, 2/1 RC, p4.
Row 6: K4, [p3, k3] twice.
Row 7: P3, k3, p3, 3/2 LPC, p2.
Row 8: K2, p3, k5, p3, k3.
Row 9: 3/3 RPC, 1/1 RC, p3, 3/1 LPC, p1.
Row 10: K1, p3, k4, p2, k3, p3.
Row 11: K3, p3, 2/3 LPC, p1, 3/1 LPC.
Row 12: P3, k2, p2, k6, p3.
Row 13: 3/2 LPC, p4, k2, 3/2 RPC.
Row 14: K2, p5, k4, p3, k2.
Row 15: 3/2 RPC, p4, 3/2 LPC, p2.
Row 16: K2, p3, k8, p3.
Row 17: 2/1 LC, p6, 3/2 RPC, p2.
Row 18: K4, p3, k6, p2, k1.
Row 19: P1, 1/1 RC, p3, 3/3 RC, p4.
Row 20: Repeat Row 4.
Repeat Rows 3 to 20.

CHART KEY:

Set-up rows (work once only)	RS: knit WS: purl	16-stitch repeat	RS: purl WS: knit

3/3 RPC

2/1 RC

3/2 LPC

1/1 RC

3/1 LPC

2/3 LPC

3/2 RPC

2/1 LC

3/3 RC

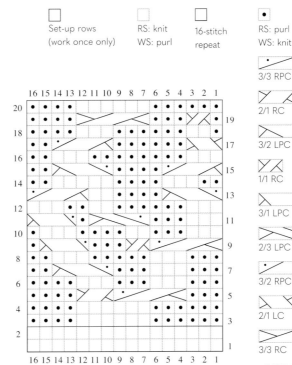

CHAPTER THREE

All-over Panels

Continuing with our cable combinations we move on to ways to use simple, single cables to create more complex, larger panels. More infills and intersecting cables give you lots of scope for experimenting with cables that can be used as all-over patterns for garments or homewares.

Wheatear

Plain cables switch with twists to create an appearance of ears of wheat waving in the summer sun.

Skill level:

SEC: 13 sts should be added per 4in (10cm) finished width

Mix & match:
Stitches Multiple of 11 sts
Repeat 32-row pattern repeat

Row 1 (RS): P1, k4, p6.
Row 2 (WS): K6, p4, k1.
Rows 3 to 6: Repeat Rows 1 and 2.
Row 7: P1, 4/1/4 LC, p1.
Row 8: K1, p9, k1.
Row 9: P1, 2/2 RC, k1, 2/2 LC, p1.
Rows 10 to 15: Repeat Rows 8 and 9.

Row 16: Repeat Row 8.
Row 17: P6, k4, p1.
Row 18: K1, p4, k6.
Rows 19 to 22: Repeat Rows 17 and 18.
Row 23: P1, 4/1/4 RC, p1.
Row 24: Repeat Row 8.

Row 25: Repeat Row 9.
Rows 26 to 31: Repeat Rows 24 and 25.
Row 32: Repeat Row 8.
Repeat Rows 1 to 32.

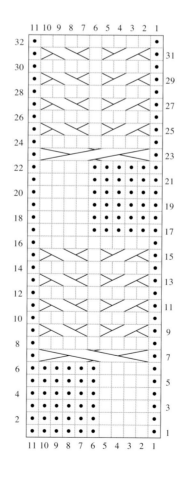

CHART KEY:

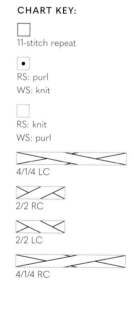

11-stitch repeat

RS: purl
WS: knit

RS: knit
WS: purl

4/1/4 LC

2/2 RC

2/2 LC

4/1/4 RC

SEC: 9 sts should be added per 4in (10cm) finished width

Mix & match:
Stitches Multiple of 7 sts
Repeat 20-row pattern repeat

Spindles

Classically elegant, this spindle cable could be worked as part of a panel but would look lovely down a sleeve or as an edging.

Row 1 (RS): [K1, p1] 3 times, k1.
Row 2 (WS): [P1, k1] 3 times, p1.
Row 3: 3/1/3 LPC.
Row 4: P3, k1, p3.
Row 5: K3, p1, k3.
Row 6: Repeat Row 4.
Row 7: 3/1/3 LPC.
Rows 8 to 11: Repeat Rows 4 to 7.
Row 12: Repeat Row 2.
Row 13: Repeat Row 1.
Rows 14 to 19: Repeat Rows 12 and 13.
Row 20: Repeat Row 2.
Repeat Rows 1 to 20.

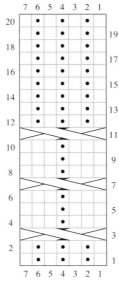

CHART KEY:

7-stitch repeat

RS: knit
WS: purl

• RS: purl
WS: knit

3/1/3 LPC

Skill level:

SEC: 8 sts should be added per 4in (10cm) finished width

Mix & match:
Stitches Multiple of 11 sts
Repeat 11-row pattern repeat

Radio Waves

This straightforward pattern has just two cables worked on the same row. The extra interest is generated by incorporating rib stitches into the repeat. It would look great as a single panel down a sleeve or as an edging, but is soft enough to produce an all-over pattern, too.

Row 1 (RS): P1, k2, p2, k1, p2, k2, p1.
Row 2 (WS): K1, p2, k2, p1, k2, p2, k1.
Rows 3 to 8: Repeat Rows 1 and 2.
Row 9: P1, 2/2 LC, k1, 2/2 RC, p1.
Row 10: K1, p9, k1.
Repeat Rows 1 to 10.

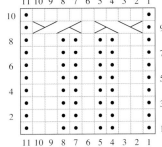

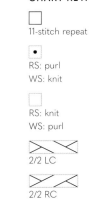

CHART KEY:

☐
11-stitch repeat

•
RS: purl
WS: knit

☐
RS: knit
WS: purl

2/2 LC

2/2 RC

Skill level:

SEC: 6 sts should be added per 4in (10cm) finished width

Mix & match:
Stitches Multiple of 10 sts
Repeat 18-row pattern repeat

Wicker Basket

A delicate single twist makes an intricate cable, adding rich detail but without being too dense, making it light enough for an all-over panel.

Row 1 (RS): K1, p3, k2, p3, k1.
Row 2 (WS): P1, k3, p2, k3, p1.
Row 3: K1, p2, 1/1 RPC, 1/1 LPC, p2, k1.
Row 4: [P1, k2] 3 times, p1.
Row 5: K1, p1, 1/1 RPC, p2, 1/1 LPC, p1, k1.
Row 6: P1, k1, p1, k4, p1, k1, p1.
Row 7: K1, 1/1 RPC, p4, 1/1 LPC, k1.
Row 8: P2, k6, p2.
Row 9: 1/1 RC, p6, 1/1 LC.
Row 10: [P2, k2] twice, p2.
Row 11: 1/1 LPC, p2, k2, p2, 1/1 RPC.
Row 12: K1, p1, k2, p2, k2, p1, k1.
Row 13: P1, 1/1 LPC, p1, k2, p1, 1/1 RPC, p1.
Row 14: K2, p1, k1, p2, k1, p1, k2.
Row 15: P2, 1/1 LPC, k2, 1/1 RPC, p2.
Row 16: K3, p4, k3.
Row 17: P3, 1/1 LPC, 1/1 RPC, p3.
Row 18: K4, p2, k4.
Repeat Rows 1 to 18.

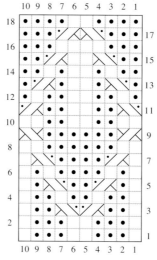

CHART KEY:

10-stitch repeat

RS: knit
WS: purl

•
RS: purl
WS: knit

1/1 RPC

1/1 LPC

1/1 RC

1/1 LC

Skill level:

SEC: 9 sts should be added per 4in (10cm) finished width

Mix & match:
Stitches Multiple of 8 sts
Repeat 8-row pattern repeat

Low Tide

This richly textured fabric is created from just two simple cables in two rows. It makes a sumptuous all-over design but can be split into a smaller repeat for combining with other stitches.

Row 1 (RS): Knit.
Row 2 and all WS rows: Purl.
Row 3: K2, 2/2 RC, k2.
Row 5: Knit.
Row 7: 2/2 LC, k4.
Row 8: Purl.
Repeat Rows 1 to 8.

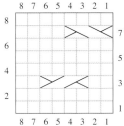

CHART KEY:

8-stitch repeat

RS: knit
WS: purl

2/2 RC

2/2 LC

Fretwork Grille

Rich, bold cable diamonds intersect on a background cross of stockinette stitch.

Skill level:

SEC: 0 sts should be added per 4in (10cm) finished width

Mix & match:
Stitches Multiple of 12 sts plus 12
Repeat 20-row pattern repeat

Row 1 (RS): P3, 2/1 RC, 2/1 LC, *p2, k2, p2, 2/1 RC, 2/1 LC; repeat from * to last 3 sts, p3.

Row 2 (WS): K3, p2, *p4, [k2, p2] twice; repeat from * to last 7 sts, p4, k3.

Row 3: P2, 2/1 RPC, k2, *2/1 LPC, p1, k2, p1, 2/1 RPC, k2; repeat from * to last 5 sts, 2/1 LPC, p2.

Row 4: K2, p2, k1, *[p2, k1] 4 times; repeat from * to last 7 sts, p2, k1, p2, k2.

Row 5: P1, 2/1 RPC, p1, k2, *p1, 2/1 LPC, k2, 2/1 RPC, p1, k2; repeat from * to last 5 sts, p1, 2/1 LPC, p1.

Row 6: K1, p2, k2, *p2, k2, p6, k2; repeat from * to last 7 sts, p2, k2, p2, k1.

Row 7: 2/1 RPC, p2, k2, *p2, 2/1 LPC, 2/1 RPC, p2, k2; repeat from * to last 5 sts, p2, 2/1 LPC.

Row 8: Purl.

Row 9: K7, *k3, 2/2 LC, k5; repeat from * to last 5 sts, k5.

Row 10: Purl.

Row 11: 2/1 LPC, p2, k2, *p2, 2/1 RC, 2/1 LC, p2, k2; repeat from * to last 5 sts, p2, 2/1 RPC.

Row 12: Repeat Row 6.

Row 13: P1, 2/1 LPC, p1, k2, *p1, 2/1 RPC, k2, 2/1 LPC, p1, k2; repeat from * to last 5 sts, p1, 2/1 RPC, p1.

Row 14: Repeat Row 4.

Row 15: P2, 2/1 LPC, k2, *2/1 RPC, p1, k2, p1, 2/1 LPC, k2; repeat from * to last 5 sts, 2/1 RPC, p2.

Row 16: Repeat Row 2.

Row 17: P3, 2/1 LPC, *2/1 RPC, p2, k2, p2, 2/1 LPC; repeat from * to last 6 sts, 2/1 RPC, p3.

Row 18: K4, p2, *[p2, k3] twice, p2; repeat from * to last 6 sts, p2, k4.

Row 19: P4, *2/2 RC, p3, k2, p3; repeat from * to last 8 sts, 2/2 RC, p4.

Row 20: Repeat Row 18.

Repeat Rows 1 to 20.

CHART KEY:

· RS: purl WS: knit

☐ 12-stitch repeat

⬛ 2/1 LPC

2/1 RC

☐ RS: knit WS: purl

2/2 LC

2/1 LC

2/1 RPC

2/2 RC

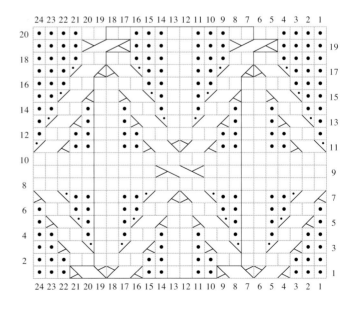

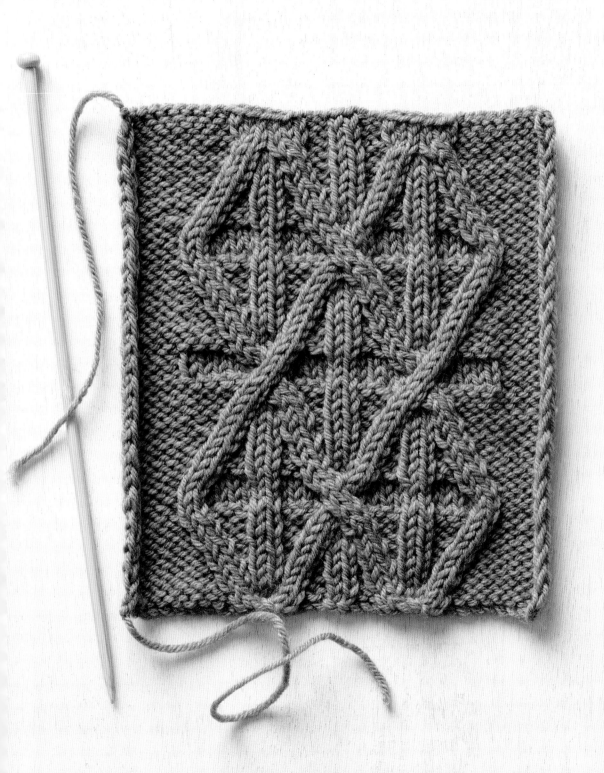

SEC: 29 sts should be added per 4in (10cm) finished width

Mix & match:
Stitches Multiple of 15 sts
Repeat 12-row pattern repeat

Syncopated Cable

Narrow chains of single twisted cables snake their way sinuously around wider cables to produce an interesting all-over design.

Row 1 (WS): [K1, p1, k1, p3] twice, k1, p1, k1.
Row 2 (RS): [P1, k1, p1, k3] twice, p1, k1, p1.
Row 3: Repeat Row 1.
Rows 4 and 5: Repeat Rows 2 and 3.
Row 6: K3, [3/3 LPKP] twice.
Row 7: [P3, k1, p1, k1] twice, p3.
Row 8: [K3, p1, k1, p1] twice, k3.
Row 9: Repeat Row 7.
Rows 10 and 11: Repeat Rows 8 and 9.
Row 12: [3/3 RPKP] twice, p1, k1, p1.
Repeat Rows 1 to 12.

Special stitches

3/3 RPKP: Slip next 3 stitches to cable needle and hold to back of work. P1, k1, p1 from LH needle. Knit 3 stitches from cable needle.

3/3 LPKP: Slip next 3 stitches to cable needle and hold to front of work. P1, k1, p1 from LH needle. Knit 3 stitches from cable needle.

CHART KEY:

15-stitch repeat

RS: purl
WS: knit

RS: knit
WS: purl

3/3 RPKP

3/3 LPKP

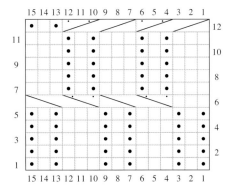

Skill level:

SEC: 1 st should be deducted per 4in (10cm) finished width

Mix & match:
Stitches Multiple of 6 sts plus 4
Repeat 12-row pattern repeat

Twin Lattice

Paired single-twist cables make an intricate lattice and create a plump, textured fabric. This stitch would make lovely homewares such as afghans or pillow covers.

Row 1 and all WS rows: Purl.

Row 2 (RS): *1/1 LC, [1/1 RC] twice; repeat from * to last 4 sts, 1/1 LC, 1/1 RC.

Row 4: K1, *1/1 LC, 1/1 RC, 1/1 LC; repeat from * to last 3 sts, 1/1 LC, k1.

Row 6: *[1/1 LC] twice, k2; repeat from * to last 4 sts, [1/1 LC] twice.

Row 8: K1, *[1/1 LC] twice, 1/1 RC; repeat from * to last 3 sts, 1/1 LC, k1.

Row 10: 1/1 RC, *1/1 LC, [1/1 RC] twice; repeat from * to last 2 sts, 1/1 LC.

Row 12: K1, *k2, [1/1 RC] twice; repeat from * to last 3 sts, k3.

Repeat Rows 1 to 12.

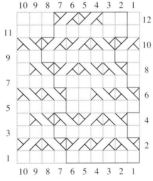

CHART KEY:

6-stitch repeat

RS: knit
WS: purl

1/1 LC

1/1 RC

Candy Canes

Thick, luscious cables entwine to create this richly textured pattern, which makes a great all-over design.

Skill level:

SEC: 9 sts should be added per 4in (10cm) finished width

Mix & match:
Stitches Multiple of 20 sts
Repeat 24-row pattern repeat

Row 1 (RS): P4, k12, p4.

Row 2 (WS): K4, p12, k4.

Row 3: P4, 4/1/1 RPC, 4/1/1 LPC, p4.

Row 4: K4, p4, k1, p2, k1, p4, k4.

Row 5: P4, k4, p1, 1/1 LC, p1, k4, p4.

Row 6: Repeat Row 4.

Row 7: P2, 4/2 RPC, p1, 1/1 LC, p1, 4/2 LPC, p2.

Row 8: K2, p4, k3, p2, k3, p4, k2.

Row 9: P2, k4, p3, 1/1 LC, p3, k4, p2.

Row 10: Repeat Row 8.

Row 11: 4/2 RPC, p3, 1/1 LC, p3, 4/2 LPC.

Row 12: P4, k5, p2, k5, p4.

Row 13: K4, p5, 1/1 LC, p5, k4.

Row 14: Repeat Row 12.

Row 15: 4/2 LPC, p3, 1/1 LC, p3, 4/2 RPC.

Row 16: Repeat Row 8.

Row 17: P2, k4, p3, 1/1 LC, p3, k4, p2.

Row 18: Repeat Row 8.

Row 19: P2, 4/2 LPC, p1, 1/1 LC, p1, 4/2 RPC, p2.

Row 20: Repeat Row 4.

Row 21: Repeat Row 5.

Row 22: Repeat Row 4.

Row 23: P4, 4/2 LPC, 4/2 RPC, p4.

Row 24: K6, p8, k6.

Row 25: P6, k8, p6.

Row 26: Repeat Row 24.

Repeat Rows 3 to 26.

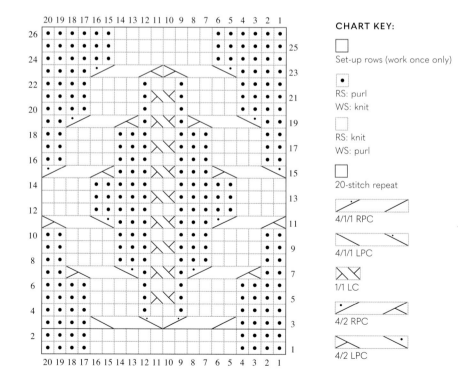

CHART KEY:

Set-up rows (work once only)

• RS: purl
WS: knit

RS: knit
WS: purl

20-stitch repeat

4/1/1 RPC

4/1/1 LPC

1/1 LC

4/2 RPC

4/2 LPC

SEC: 2 sts should be added per 4in (10cm) finished width

Mix & match:
Stitches Multiple of 6 sts plus 3
Repeat 4-row pattern repeat

Basketweave

Just two straightforward cables are worked close together to give a sturdy fabric, which is great for bags, homewares, and accessories. For a softer alternative, add extra "rest rows" between the cables.

Row 1 (RS): 3/3 LC to last 3 sts, k3.
Row 2 (WS): Purl.
Row 3: K3, 3/3 RC to end of row.
Row 4: Purl.
Repeat Rows 1 to 4.

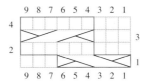

CHART KEY:

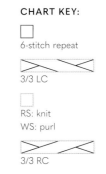

6-stitch repeat

3/3 LC

RS: knit
WS: purl

3/3 RC

Skill level: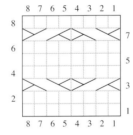

SEC: 9 sts should be added per 4in (10cm) finished width

Mix & match:
Stitches Multiple of 8 sts
Repeat 8-row pattern repeat

Honeycomb

A classic honeycomb fabric with deep texture and a springy, full drape. Traditionally worked as a wide panel or all-over fabric, the short stitch repeat means it also combines well as part of a larger design.

Row 1 (RS): Knit.
Row 2 and all WS rows: Purl.
Row 3: 2/2 RC, 2/2 LC.
Row 5: Knit.
Row 7: 2/2 LC, 2/2 RC.
Row 8: Purl.
Repeat Rows 1 to 8.

CHART KEY:

8-stitch repeat

RS: knit
WS: purl

2/2 RC

2/2 LC

Skill level: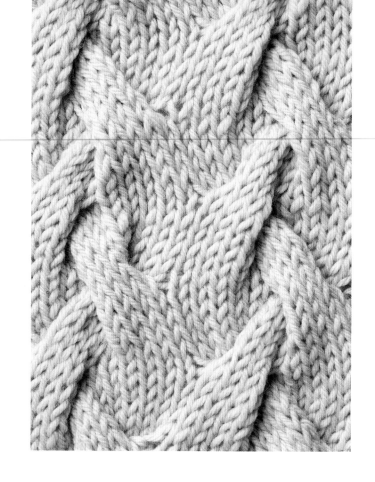

SEC: 9 sts should be added per 4in (10cm) finished width

Mix & match:
Stitches Multiple of 15 sts
Repeat 12-row pattern repeat

Ocean Waves

A beautifully delicate, undulating effect that makes a fabulous all-over pattern. The wide, 10-stitch cables are a little fiddly to work but with only two cables in the 12-row repeat there is time to relax in between!

Row 1 (RS): Knit.
Row 2 and all WS rows: Purl.
Row 3: 5/5 LC, k5.
Row 5: Knit.
Row 7: Knit.
Row 9: K5, 5/5 RC.
Row 11: Knit.
Row 12: Purl.
Repeat Rows 1 to 12.

CHART KEY:

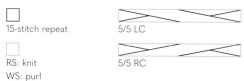

15-stitch repeat

5/5 LC

RS: knit
WS: purl

5/5 RC

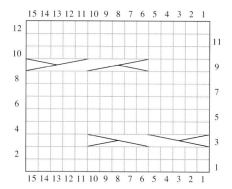

Skill level: ⬤ ⬤ ⬤

SEC: 38 sts should be added per 4in (10cm) finished width

Mix & match:
Stitches Multiple of 28 sts
Repeat 16-row pattern repeat

Twin Hourglass

A simple hourglass cable is enhanced with a central cable section for an interesting, detailed design.

Row 1 (WS): *K4, p1, k1, p2, k1, p1, k5, p1, k1, p1, k2, p2, k2, [p1, k1]twice; repeat from * to end.

Row 2 (RS): *P1, [1/1 LPC] twice, 1/1 RPC, 1/1 LPC, [1/1 RPC] twice, p4, [1/1 RPC] twice, [1/1 LPC] twice, p3; repeat from * to end.

Row 3: *K3, p1, k1, p1, k2, p1, k1, p1, k5, p1, k1, p2, k2, p2, k1, p1, k2; repeat from * to end.

Row 4: *P2, [1/1 LPC] twice, p2, [1/1 RPC] twice, p4, 1/1 RPC, 1/1 RC, p2, 1/1 LC, 1/1 LPC, p2; repeat from * to end.

Row 5: *K2, p1, k1, p2, k2, p2, k1, p1, k5, p1, k1, p1, k2, p1, k1, p1, k3; repeat from * to end.

Row 6: *P3, [1/1 LPC] twice, [1/1 RPC] twice, p4, [1/1 RPC] twice, 1/1 LPC, 1/1 RPC, [1/1 LPC] twice, p1; repeat from * to end.

Row 7: *[K1, p1] twice, k2, p2, k2, p1, k1, p1, k5, p1, k1, p2, k1, p1, k4; repeat from * to end.

Row 8: *P4, k1, p1, k2, p1, k1, p5, k1, p1, k1, p2, k2, p2, [k1, p1] twice; repeat from * to end.

Row 9: Repeat Row 7.

Row 10: *P3, [1/1 RPC] twice, [1/1 LPC] twice, p4, [1/1 LPC] twice, 1/1 RPC, 1/1 LPC, [1/1 RPC] twice, p1; repeat from * to end.

Row 11: Repeat Row 5.

Row 12: *P2, 1/1 RPC, 1/1 RC, p2, 1/1 LC, 1/1 LPC, p4, [1/1 LPC] twice, p2, [1/1 RPC] twice, p2; repeat from * to end.

Row 13: Repeat Row 3.

Row 14: *P1, [1/1 RPC] twice, 1/1 LPC, 1/1 RPC, [1/1 LPC] twice, p4, [1/1 LPC] twice, [1/1 RPC] twice, p3 ; repeat from * to end.

Row 15: Repeat Row 1.

Row 16: *[P1, k1] twice, p2, k2, p2, k1, p1, k1, p5, k1, p1, k2, p1, k1, p4; repeat from * to end.

Repeat Rows 1 to 16.

CHART KEY:

☐ 28-stitch repeat	☐ RS: knit WS: purl	⟋ 1/1 RPC
• RS: purl WS: knit	⟋ 1/1 LPC	⟍ 1/1 RC
		⟍ 1/1 LC

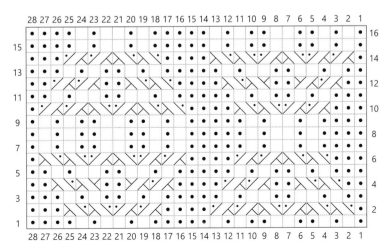

Garter Diamonds

Placing cables on a garter stitch background gives a springy feel without losing the definition of the classic cable diamond.

Row 1 (RS): K3, 2/1 RC, 2/1 LC, k3.
Row 2 (WS): K3, p2, k2, p2, k3.
Row 3: K2, 2/1 RC, k2, 2/1 LC, k2.
Row 4: K2, p2, k4, p2, k2.
Row 5: K1, 2/1 RC, k4, 2/1 LC, k1.
Row 6: K1, p2, k6, p2, k1.
Row 7: 2/1 RC, k6, 2/1 LC.
Row 8: P2, k8, p2.
Row 9: 2/1 LC, k6, 2/1 RC.
Row 10: Repeat Row 6.
Row 11: K1, 2/1 LC, k4, 2/1 RC, k1.
Row 12: Repeat Row 4.
Row 13: K2, 2/1 LC, k2, 2/1 RC, k2.
Row 14: Repeat Row 2.
Row 15: K3, 2/1 LC, 2/1 RC, k3.
Row 16: K4, p4, k4.
Repeat Rows 1 to 16.

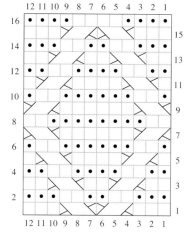

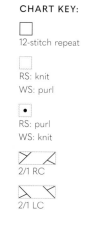

CHART KEY:

12-stitch repeat

RS: knit
WS: purl

• RS: purl
WS: knit

2/1 RC

2/1 LC

Skill level:

SEC: 2 sts should be added per 4in (10cm) finished width

Mix & match:
Stitches Multiple of 16 sts plus 2
Repeat 24-row pattern repeat

Seed Stitch Checkers

A playful design that combines seed (moss) stitch and two simple cables in symmetrical blocks. This works up into a comfortable, soft fabric. To produce a sturdier fabric for homewares, use needles one or two sizes smaller than normal.

Row 1 (RS): K8, [p1, k1] 4 times.
Row 2 (WS): [K1, p1] 3 times, k1, p9.
Rows 3 to 6: Repeat Rows 1 and 2.
Row 7: 4/4 LC, [p1, k1] 4 times.
Row 8: Repeat Row 2.
Row 9: Repeat Row 1.
Rows 10 and 11: Repeat Rows 8 and 9.
Row 12: Repeat Row 2.
Row 13: [K1, p1] 4 times, k8.
Row 14: P9, [k1, p1] 3 times, k1.
Rows 15 to 18: Repeat Rows 13 and 14.
Row 19: [K1, p1] 4 times, 4/4 RC.
Row 20: Repeat Row 14.
Row 21: Repeat Row 13.
Rows 22 and 23: Repeat Rows 20 and 21.
Row 24: Repeat Row 14.
Repeat Rows 1 to 24.

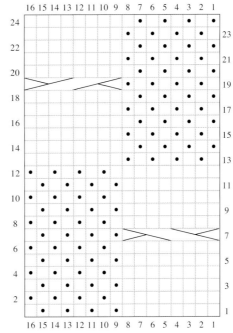

CHART KEY:

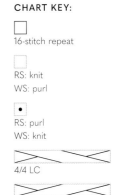

16-stitch repeat

RS: knit
WS: purl

• RS: purl
WS: knit

4/4 LC

4/4 RC

Cords and Diamonds

There is quite a lot going on with this more complex cable, but the end result is elegant and stylish, making it worth the extra effort!

Skill level:

SEC: 7 sts should be added per 4in (10cm) finished width

Mix & match:
Stitches Multiple of 12 sts plus 16
Repeat 16-row pattern repeat

Row 1 (RS): P1, 1/1 RC, p2, 2/1 RPC, 2/1 LPC, *p2, 1/1 RC, p2, 2/1 RPC, 2/1 LPC; repeat from * to last 5 sts, p2, 1/1 RC, p1.

Row 2 (WS): K1, p2, k2, p2, * [k2, p2] 3 times; repeat from * to last 9 sts, [k2, p2] twice, k1.

Row 3: P1, 1/1 RC, p1, 2/1 RPC, p2, *2/1 LPC, p1, 1/1 RC, p1, 2/1 RPC, p2; repeat from * to last 7 sts, 2/1 LPC, p1, 1/1 RC, p1.

Row 4: [K1, p2] twice, k1, *k3, [p2, k1] 3 times; repeat from * to last 9 sts, k3, [p2, k1] twice.

Row 5: P1, 1/1 RC, 2/1 RPC, p3, *p1, 2/1 LPC, 1/1 RC, 2/1 RPC, p3; repeat from * to last 7 sts, p1, 2/1 LPC, 1/1 RC, p1.

Row 6: K1, p4, k2, *k4, p6, k2; repeat from * to last 9 sts, k4, p4, k1.

Row 7: P1, k1, 2/1 RPC, p4, *p2, 2/1 LPC, 2/1 RPC, p4; repeat from * to last 7 sts, p2, 2/1 LPC, k1, p1.

Row 8: K1, p3, k3, *k5, p4, k3; repeat from * to last 9 sts, k5, p3, k1.

Row 9: P1, k1, 2/1 LC, p4, *p2, 2/1 RC, 2/1 LC, p4; repeat from * to last 7 sts, p2, 2/1 RC, k1, p1.

Row 10: Repeat Row 6.

Row 11: P1, 1/1 RC, 2/1 LPC, p3, *p1, 2/1 RPC, 1/1 RC, 2/1 LPC, p3; repeat from * to last 7 sts, p1, 2/1 RPC, 1/1 RC, p1.

Row 12: Repeat Row 4.

Row 13: P1, 1/1 RC, p1, 2/1 LPC, p2, *2/1 RPC, p1, 1/1 RC, p1, 2/1 LPC, p2; repeat from * to last 7 sts, 2/1 RPC, p1, 1/1 RC, p1.

Row 14: Repeat Row 2.

Row 15: P1, 1/1 RC, p2, 2/1 LPC, *2/1 RPC, p2, 1/1 RC, p2, 2/1 LPC; repeat from * to last 8 sts, 2/1 RPC, p2, 1/1 RC, p1.

Row 16: K1, p2, k3, p2, *[p2, k3] twice, p2; repeat from * to last 8 sts, p2, k3, p2, k1.

Repeat Rows 1 to 16.

CHART KEY:

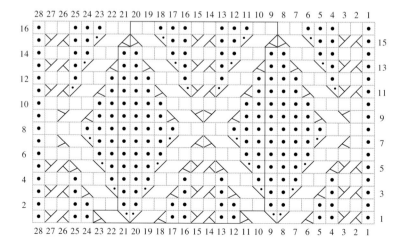

Skill level:

SEC: 5 sts should be added per 4in (10cm) finished width

Mix & match:
Stitches Multiple of 8 sts plus 2
Repeat 10-row pattern repeat

Mill Windows

A bold, geometric design that works well as an all-over pattern but could be used as a single repeat combined with other stitches. The garter stitch really makes the cable stitches "pop."

Row 1 (RS): Knit.
Row 2 and all WS rows: Purl.
Row 3: P1, *p2, k4, p2; repeat from * to last st, p1.
Row 5: Repeat Row 3.
Row 7: Repeat Row 3.
Row 9: K1, *k2, p4, k2; repeat from * to last st, k1.
Row 11: K1, *2/2 LC, 2/2 RC; repeat from * to last st, k1.
Repeat Rows 2 to 11.

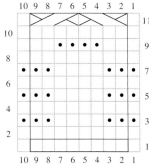

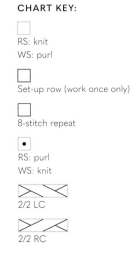

CHART KEY:

RS: knit
WS: purl

Set-up row (work once only)

8-stitch repeat

RS: purl
WS: knit

2/2 LC

2/2 RC

SEC: 2 sts should be added per 4in (10cm) finished width

Mix & match:
Stitches Multiple of 4 sts plus 2
Repeat 8-row pattern repeat

Rippling Sand

This pattern appears complex but it is simply the addition of slipped stitches below the cables that creates the extra texture, giving it the illusion of ripples on the sand.

Row 1 (RS): K1, *slwyib, k3; repeat from * to last st, k1.
Row 2 (WS): P1, *p3, slwyif; repeat from * to last st, p1.
Row 3: K1, *1/2 LC, k1; repeat from * to last st, k1.
Row 4: Purl.
Row 5: K1, *k3, slwyib; repeat from * to last st, k1.
Row 6: P1, *slwyif, p3; repeat from * to last st, p1.
Row 7: K1, *k1, 1/2 RC; repeat from * to last st, k1.
Row 8: Purl.
Repeat Rows 1 to 8.

Special stitches

slwyib: Slip purlwise with yarn in back.
slwyif: Slip purlwise with yarn in front.

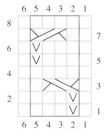

CHART KEY:

RS: knit
WS: purl

4-stitch repeat

V
RS: slwyib
WS: slwyif

1/2 LC

1/2 RC

CHAPTER FOUR

Creative Cables

In this chapter we take our explorations further with the addition of colorwork, lace, and bobbles for texture. We also look at some very useful reversible cables that are ideal for scarves, wraps, and other garments where both sides of the project will be visible.

Skill level:

SEC: 9 sts should be added per 4in (10cm) finished width

Mix & match:
Stitches Multiple of 16 sts
Repeat 8-row pattern repeat

Snaking Reversible Cable

Two classic rope cables are made to look much more intricate simply by offsetting them, creating a subtle, snaking effect.

Row 1 (RS): *[K2, p2] 4 times; repeat from * to end.

Row 2 and all WS rows: *[K2, p2] 4 times; repeat from * to end.

Row 3: *4/4 LRC, [k2, p2] twice; repeat from * to end.

Row 5: Repeat Row 1.

Row 7: *[K2, p2] twice, 4/4 RRC; repeat from * to end.

Row 8: Repeat Row 2.

Repeat Rows 1 to 8.

Special stitches

4/4 LRC: Slip next 4 stitches to cable needle and place at front of work. K2, p2. K2, p2 from cable needle.

4/4 RRC: Slip next 4 stitches to cable needle and place at back of work. K2, p2. K2, p2 from cable needle.

CHART KEY:

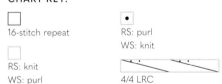

16-stitch repeat

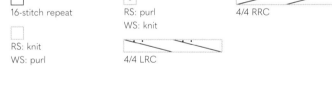

RS: purl
WS: knit

4/4 RRC

RS: knit
WS: purl

4/4 LRC

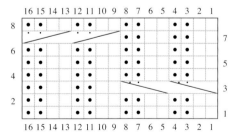

Skill level:

SEC: 5 sts should be added per 4in (10cm) finished width

Mix & match:
Stitches Multiple of 15 sts plus 5
Repeat 30-row pattern repeat

Threaded Cable

This stitch creates a fascinating optical illusion that looks particularly dramatic when worked over a large area of fabric.

Row 1 (WS): K5, *k10, p2, k1, p2; repeat from * to end.

Row 2 (RS): *K2, p1, k2, p10; repeat from * to last 5 sts, p5.

Row 3: Repeat Row 1.

Rows 4 to 9: Repeat Rows 2 and 3.

Row 10: *5/5 RPRC, p5; repeat from * to last 5 sts, p5.

Row 11: K5, *k5, p2, k1, p2, k5; repeat from * to end.

Row 12: *P5, k2, p1, k2, p5; repeat from * to last 5 sts, p5.

Row 13: Repeat Row 11.

Rows 14 to 19: Repeat Rows 12 and 13.

Row 20: *P5, 5/5 RPRC; repeat from * to last 5 sts, p5.

Row 21: K5, *p2, k1, p2, k10; repeat from * to end.

Row 22: *P10, k2, p1, k2; repeat from * to last 5 sts, p5.

Row 23: Repeat Row 21.

Rows 24 to 29: Repeat Rows 22 and 23.

Row 30: P5, *p5, 5/5 RPRC; repeat from * to end.

Repeat Rows 1 to 30.

Special stitches

5/5 RPRC: Slip next 5 stitches to cable needle and place at back of work. P5 from LH needle, k2, p1, k2 from cable needle.

CHART KEY:

15-stitch repeat

RS: knit
WS: purl

• RS: purl
WS: knit

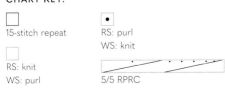

5/5 RPRC

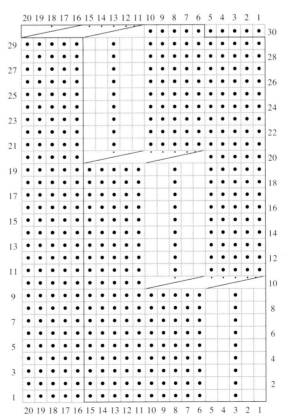

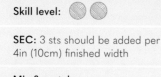

Twining Two-color Garter

Adding both color and texture to a straightforward cable gives it real impact.

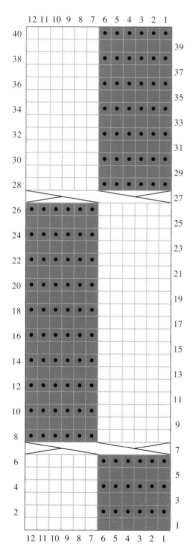

CHART KEY:

☐ 12-stitch repeat

☐ RS: knit
WS: purl

• RS: purl
WS: knit

⧖ 6/6 LC

☐ Color A

▦ Color B

Cast on in color A and use chart to follow color changes.

Row 1 (RS): Knit.

Row 2 (WS): *P6, k6; repeat from * to end.

Rows 3 to 6: Repeat Rows 1 and 2.

Row 7: *6/6 LC; repeat from * to end.

Row 8: *K6, p6; repeat from * to end.

Row 9: Knit.

Rows 10 to 25: Repeat Rows 8 and 9.

Row 26: Repeat Row 8.

Row 27: *6/6 LC; repeat from * to end.

Row 28: Repeat Row 2.

Row 29: Knit.

Rows 30 to 39: Repeat Rows 28 and 29.

Row 40: Repeat Row 2.

Repeat Rows 1 to 40.

SEC: 1 st should be added per 4in (10cm) finished width

Mix & match:
Stitches Multiple of 8 sts plus 2
Repeat 20-row pattern repeat

Seed and Lace Window

This richly textured cable is combined with seed (moss) stitch and lacy eyelets. It would make a lovely all-over panel as the fabric is complex but retains its softness and drape due to the lacy yarnovers.

Row 1 (RS): *[P1, k1] 4 times; repeat from * to end.

Row 2 (WS): *[K1, p1] 4 times; repeat from * to end.

Rows 3 to 6: Repeat Rows 1 and 2.

Row 7: Knit.

Row 8: Purl.

Rows 9 and 10: Repeat Rows 7 and 8.

Row 11: *2/2 LC, 2/2 RC; repeat from * to end.

Row 12: Purl.

Row 13: Knit.

Row 14: Purl.

Row 15: *1/1 LC, 1/1 RC; repeat from * to end.

Row 16: Purl.

Row 17: K1, *yo, k2tog; repeat from * to last st, k1.

Row 18: Purl.

Row 19: Knit.

Row 20: Purl.

Repeat Rows 1 to 20.

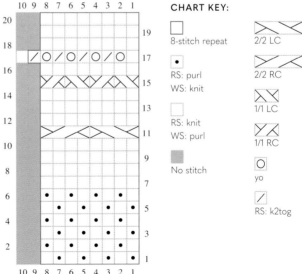

CHART KEY:

□ 8-stitch repeat	⟩⟨ 2/2 LC	
• RS: purl / WS: knit	⟩⟨ 2/2 RC	
□ RS: knit / WS: purl	⟩⟨ 1/1 LC	
▨ No stitch	⟩⟨ 1/1 RC	
	O yo	
	╱ RS: k2tog	

SEC: 6 sts should be added per 4in (10cm) finished width

Mix & match:
Stitches Multiple of 8 sts
Repeat 16-row pattern repeat

Seed and Stockinette

The knobbly texture of the seed (moss) stitch makes the paired stockinette strand really pop. This stitch would look dramatic worked alongside a mirrored cable using left-twisting stitches.

Row 1 (RS): *P1, k1, p1, k5; repeat from * to end.
Row 2 (WS): *P4, [k1, p1] twice; repeat from * to end.
Rows 3 and 4: Repeat Rows 1 and 2.
Row 5: *4/4 RCSS; repeat from * to end.
Row 7: *K4, [p1, k1] twice; repeat from * to end.
Rows 8 to 11: Repeat Rows 6 and 7.
Row 12: Repeat Row 6.
Row 13: *4/4 SSRC; repeat from * to end.
Row 14: *P4, [k1, p1] twice; repeat from * to end.
Row 15: Repeat Row 1.
Row 16: Repeat Row 2.
Repeat Rows 1 to 16.

Special stitches

4/4 RCSS: Place next 4 stitches on cable needle and hold at back of work, k4, then [p1, k1] twice from cable needle.
4/4 SSRC: Slip next 4 stitches to cable needle and place at back of work, [p1, k1] twice, then k4 from cable needle.

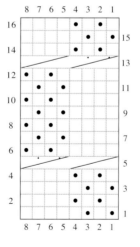

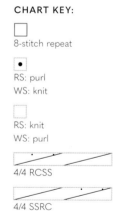

CHART KEY:

8-stitch repeat

• RS: purl
WS: knit

RS: knit
WS: purl

4/4 RCSS

4/4 SSRC

Skill level: ●●

SEC: 3 sts should be added per 4in (10cm) finished width

Mix & match:
Stitches Multiple of 15 sts
Repeat 16-row pattern repeat

Seed and Garter Reversible Cable

Although there's lots going on with this cable, the garter stitch background makes a strong contrast against the cable with a seed (moss) stitch center.

Row 1 (RS): *K7, p1, k7; repeat from * to end.
Row 2 and all WS rows: *K3, p3, k1, p1, k1, p3, k3; repeat from * to end.
Row 3: Repeat Row 1.
Row 5: Repeat Row 1.
Row 7: *K3, 3/3/3 SSLC, k3; repeat from * to end.
Row 9: Repeat Row 1.
Row 11: Repeat Row 1.
Row 13: Repeat Row 1.
Row 15: Repeat Row 1.
Row 16: Repeat Row 2.
Repeat Rows 1 to 16.

Special stitch

3/3/3 SSLC: Slip next 6 stitches to cable needle and hold at front of work, k3, then move 3 stitches from the cable needle back to the LH needle, k1, p1, k1, then k3 from cable needle.

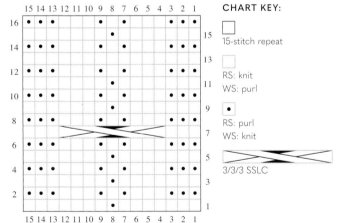

CHART KEY:

☐ 15-stitch repeat

☐ RS: knit
WS: purl

• RS: purl
WS: knit

✕ 3/3/3 SSLC

Skill level: ◉ ◉ ◉

SEC: 3 sts should be added per 4in (10cm) finished width

Mix & match:
Stitches Multiple of 13 sts
Repeat 16-row pattern repeat

Bobble and Seed

Colorful bobbles add a fun highlight to this seed- (moss-) stitch filled zigzag cable. Use short lengths of a second color to keep the wrong side of the work tidy, or work in the same color throughout for a more subtle look.

Cast on in color A. For colored bobbles, follow color changes as indicated in chart.

Row 1 (RS): *P3, 2/1 RPC, k1, 2/1 LPC, p3; repeat from * to end.

Row 2 (WS): *K3, p3, k1, p3, k3; repeat from * to end.

Row 3: *P2, 2/1 RC, p1, MB, p1, 2/1 LC, p2; repeat from * to end.

Row 4: *K2, p2, [k1, p1] twice, k1, p2, k2; repeat from * to end.

Row 5: *P1, 2/1 RPC, [k1, p1] twice, k1, 2/1 LPC, p1; repeat from * to end.

Row 6: *K1, p3, [k1, p1] twice, k1, p3, k1; repeat from * to end.

Row 7: *2/1 RC, p1, k1, p1, MB, p1, k1, p1, 2/1 LC; repeat from * to end.

Row 8: *P2, [k1, p1] 4 times, k1, p2; repeat from * to end.

Row 9: *2/1 LPC, [p1, k1] 3 times, p1, 2/1 RPC; repeat from * to end.

Row 10: Repeat Row 6.

Row 11: *P1, 2/1 LPC, k1, p1, MB, p1, k1, 2/1 RPC, p1; repeat from * to end.

Row 12: Repeat Row 4.

Row 13: *P2, 2/1 LPC, p1, k1, p1, 2/1 RPC, p2; repeat from * to end.

Row 14: Repeat Row 2.

Row 15: *P3, 2/1 LPC, k1, 2/1 RPC, p3; repeat from * to end.

Row 16: *K4, p2, k1, p2, k4; repeat from * to end.

Repeat Rows 1 to 16.

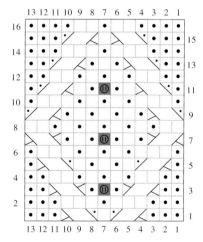

Special stitch

MB, make bobble: [K1, p1, k1, p1, k1] into 1 stitch, turn, p5, turn, slip 5 stitches to RH needle purlwise, lift stitches 2, 3, 4, 5 over to leave 1 stitch.

CHART KEY:

☐ 13-stitch repeat

• RS: purl
WS: knit

⟍ 2/1 RPC

☐ RS: knit
WS: purl

⟍ 2/1 LPC

⟋ 2/1 RC

Ⓤ MB

⟍ 2/1 LC

☐ Color A

 Color B

Skill level:

SEC: 9 sts should be added per 4in (10cm) finished width

Mix & match:
Stitches Multiple of 16 sts
Repeat 20-row pattern repeat

Cabled Cable

This cable consists of just two strands, each one popping out of the side of a regular rope cable at intervals.

Row 1 (RS): *P3, 2/2 LPC, 2/2 LC, p5; repeat from * to end.

Row 2 (WS): *K5, p6, k5; repeat from * to end.

Row 3: *P5, 2/2 RC, 2/2 LPC, p3; repeat from * to end.

Row 4: *K3, p2, k2, p4, k5; repeat from * to end.

Row 5: *P5, k4, p2, 2/2 LPC, p1; repeat from * to end.

Row 6: *K1, p2, k4, p4, k5; repeat from * to end.

Row 7: *P5, 2/2 RC, p4, k2, p1; repeat from * to end.

Row 8: Repeat Row 6.

Row 9: *P5, k4, p2, 2/2 RPC, p1; repeat from * to end.

Row 10: Repeat Row 4.

Row 11: *P5, 2/2 RC, 2/2 RPC, p3; repeat from * to end.

Row 12: Repeat Row 2.

Row 13: *P3, 2/2 RPC, 2/2 LC, p5; repeat from * to end.

Row 14: *K5, p4, k2, p2, k3; repeat from * to end.

Row 15: *P1, 2/2 RPC, p2, k4, p5; repeat from * to end.

Row 16: *K5, p4, k4, p2, k1; repeat from * to end.

Row 17: *P1, k2, p4, 2/2 LC, p5; repeat from * to end.

Row 18: Repeat Row 16.

Row 19: *P1, 2/2 LPC, p2, k4, p5; repeat from * to end.

Row 20: Repeat Row 14.

Repeat Rows 1 to 20.

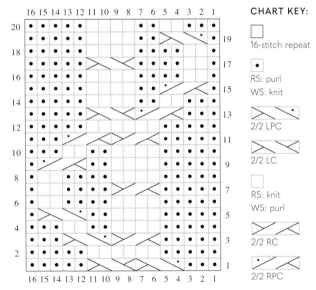

CHART KEY:

16-stitch repeat

•
RS: purl
WS: knit

2/2 LPC

2/2 LC

RS: knit
WS: purl

2/2 RC

2/2 RPC

Garter Diamond and Knot

Elegant simplicity combines two cable strands with carefully placed bobbles on a garter stitch background. The garter stitch makes a soft, fluid fabric, ideal for garments.

Skill level:

SEC: 2 sts should be added per 4in (10cm) finished width

Mix & match:
Stitches Multiple of 19 sts plus 3
Repeat 30-row pattern repeat

Row 1 (RS): *K9, 2/2 RC, k6; repeat from * to last 3 sts, k3.

Row 2 (WS): K3, *k6, p4, k9; repeat from * to end.

Row 3: *K9, 2/2 LC, k6; repeat from * to last 3 sts, k3.

Row 4: Repeat row 2.

Rows 5 to 8: Repeat Rows 1 to 4.

Row 9: *K8, 2/1 RC, 2/1 LC, k5; repeat from * to last 3 sts, k3.

Row 10: K3, *k5, p2, k2, p2, k8; repeat from * to end.

Row 11: *K7, 2/1 RC, k2, 2/1 LC, k4; repeat from * to last 3 sts, k3.

Row 12: K3, *[k4, p2] twice, k7 ; repeat from * to end.

Row 13: *K6, 2/1 RC, k4, 2/1 LC, k3; repeat from * to last 3 sts, k3.

Row 14: K3, *k3, [p2, k6] twice; repeat from * to end.

Row 15: *K5, 2/1 RC, k6, 2/1 LC, k2; repeat from * to last 3 sts, k3.

Row 16: K3, *k2, p2, k8, p2, k5; repeat from * to end.

Row 17: *K4, 2/1 RC, k8, 2/1 LC, k1; repeat from * to last 3 sts, k3.

Row 18: K3, *k1, p2, k10, p2, k4; repeat from * to end.

Row 19: *K3, mb, k14, mb; repeat from * to last 3 sts, k3.

Row 20: Repeat Row 18.

Row 21: *K4, 2/1 LC, k8, 2/1 RC, k1; repeat from * to last 3 sts, k3.

Row 22: Repeat Row 16.

Row 23: *K5, 2/1 LC, k6, 2/1 RC, k2; repeat from * to last 3 sts, k3.

Row 24: Repeat Row 14.

Row 25: *K6, 2/1 LC, k4, 2/1 RC, k3; repeat from * to last 3 sts, k3.

Row 26: Repeat Row 12.

Row 27: *K7, 2/1 LC, k2, 2/1 RC, k4; repeat from * to last 3 sts, k3.

Row 28: Repeat Row 10.

Row 29: *K8, 2/1 LC, 2/1 RC, k5; repeat from * to last 3 sts, k3.

Row 30: Repeat Row 2.

Repeat Rows 1 to 30.

Special stitch

MB, make bobble: [K1, p1, k1, p1, k1] into 1 stitch, turn, slip 5 stitches to RH needle purlwise, lift stitches 2, 3, 4, 5 over to leave 1 stitch.

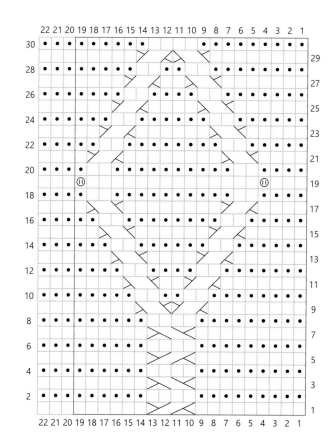

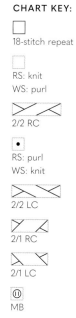

CHART KEY:

18-stitch repeat

RS: knit
WS: purl

2/2 RC

RS: purl
WS: knit

2/2 LC

2/1 RC

2/1 LC

MB

Skill level:

SEC: 2 sts should be added per 4in (10cm) finished width

Mix & match:
Stitches Multiple of 12 sts plus 2
Repeat 8-row pattern repeat

Serpents and Ladders

A wide cable combination that would be ideal as a central panel for a garment. Alternatively, it could be divided into three separate sections, with additional garter stitches inserted between the sections to make the panel wider.

Row 1 (RS): *1/1 RC, k10; repeat from * to last 2 sts, 1/1 RC.

Row 2 and all WS rows: *P6, k2, p4; repeat from * to last 2 sts, p2.

Row 3: K1, *2/2 RC, k4, 2/2 LC; repeat from * to last st, k1.

Row 5: *1/1 LC, k10; repeat from * to last 2 sts, 1/1 LC.

Row 7: *1/1 RC, k1, 2/2 LC, 2/2 RC, k1; repeat from * to last 2 sts, 1/1 RC.

Row 8: Knit.

Repeat Rows 1 to 8.

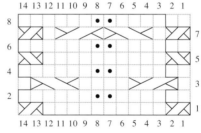

CHART KEY:

☐
12-stitch repeat

⬔
1/1 RC

☐
RS: knit
WS: purl

•
RS: purl
WS: knit

⬓
2/2 RC

⬓
2/2 LC

⬔
1/1 LC

Skill level: ⊘ ⊘

SEC: 3 sts should be deducted per 4in (10cm) finished width

Mix & match:
Stitches Multiple of 17 sts plus 8
Repeat 8-row pattern repeat

Lacy Ribbed Cable

Combining cables with other techniques, such as lace used here, can give a fabric extra interest and a completely different look.

Row 1 (RS): *[K1, p1] 4 times, k1, yo, k2tog, k3, k2tog, yo, k1; repeat from * to last 8 sts, [k1, p1] 4 times.

Row 2 and all WS rows: [K1, p1] 4 times, *p9, [k1, p1] 4 times; repeat from * to end.

Row 3: *[K1, p1] 4 times, k2, yo, k2tog, k1, k2tog, yo, k2; repeat from * to last 8 sts, [k1, p1] 4 times.

Row 5: *4/4 RCL, k3, yo, sk2po, yo, k3; repeat from * to last 8 sts, 4/4 RCR.

Row 7: *[K1, p1] 4 times, k9; repeat from * to last 8 sts, [k1, p1] 4 times.

Row 8: Repeat Row 2.

Repeat Rows 1 to 8.

Special stitches

4/4 RCL: Slip next 4 sts to cable needle and hold to front of work. K1, p1, k1, p1. K1, p1, k1, p1 from cable needle.

4/4 RCR: Slip next 4 sts to cable needle and hold to back of work. K1, p1, k1, p1. K1, p1, k1, p1 from cable needle.

CHART KEY:

☐	17-stitch repeat
☐	RS: knit / WS: purl
•	RS: purl / WS: knit
O	yo
/	k2tog
∧	sk2po
⟍	4/4 RCR
⟋	4/4 RCL

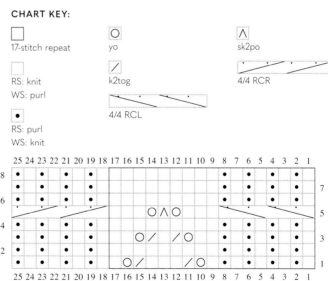

Skill level:

SEC: 3 sts should be added per 4in (10cm) finished width

Mix & match:
Stitches Multiple of 13 sts
Repeat 22-row pattern repeat

Knotted Ribeye Cable

Bobbles fill the center of this gently curving cable, adding interest and rich texture. This stitch would make a bold single panel or combine it with a simple wiggling cable.

Row 1 (RS): Knit.
Row 2 and all WS rows: Purl.
Row 3: Knit.
Row 5: 3/3 RC, MB, 3/3 LC.
Row 7: Knit.
Row 9: K3, [MB, k2] twice, MB, k3.
Row 11: Knit.
Row 13: 3/3 LC, MB, 3/3 RC.
Row 15: Knit.
Row 17: 3/3 RC, k1, 3/3 LC.
Row 19: Knit.
Row 21: 3/3 LC, k1, 3/3 RC.
Row 22: Purl.
Repeat Rows 1 to 22.

Special stitch

MB, make bobble: [K1, p1, k1, p1, k1] into 1 stitch, turn, slip 5 stitches to RH needle purlwise, lift stitches 2, 3, 4, 5 over to leave 1 stitch.

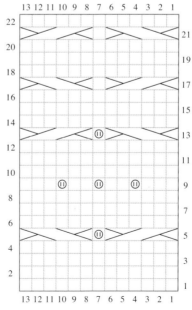

CHART KEY:

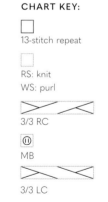

13-stitch repeat

RS: knit
WS: purl

3/3 RC

Ⓜ MB

3/3 LC

SEC: 1 st should be added per 4in (10cm) finished width

Mix & match:
Stitches Multiple of 18 sts
Repeat 18-row pattern repeat

Lacy Twin Leaf

Cables can be subtle as well as bold. Here, two-stitch cables frame a lacy fabric to create pretty leaf shapes. This produces a soft fabric suitable for all-over patterns but is equally lovely worked as a panel.

Row 1 (RS): *P5, 1/1 RC, k1, p2, k1, 1/1 LC, p5; repeat from * to end.

Row 2 (WS): *K5, p3, k2, p3, k5; repeat from * to end.

Row 3: *P4, 1/1 RC, k2tog, yo, p2, yo, skpo, 1/1 LC, p4; repeat from * to end.

Row 4: *K4, p4, k2, p4, k4; repeat from * to end.

Row 5: *P3, 1/1 RC, k2tog, yo, k1, p2, k1, yo, skpo, 1/1 LC, p3; repeat from * to end.

Row 6: *K3, p5, k2, p5, k3; repeat from * to end.

Row 7: *P2, 1/1 RC, k2tog, yo, k2, p2, k2, yo, skpo, 1/1 LC, p2; repeat from * to end.

Row 8: *[K2, p6] twice, k2; repeat from * to end.

Row 9: *P1, 1/1 RC, k3, k2tog, yo, p2, yo, skpo, k3, 1/1 LC, p1; repeat from * to end.

Row 10: *K1, p6, k4, p6, k1; repeat from * to end.

Row 11: *P1, 1/1 RC, k2, k2tog, yo, p4, yo, skpo, k2, 1/1 LC, p1; repeat from * to end.

Row 12: *K1, p5, k6, p5, k1; repeat from * to end.

Row 13: *P1, 1/1 RC, k1, k2tog, yo, p6, yo, skpo, k1, 1/1 LC, p1; repeat from * to end.

Row 14: *K1, p4, k8, p4, k1; repeat from * to end.

Row 15: *P1, 2/2 RPC, p8, 2/2 LPC, p1; repeat from * to end.

Row 16: *K1, p2, k12, p2, k1; repeat from * to end.

Row 17: *P1, 1/1 RPC, p12, 1/1 LPC, p1; repeat from * to end.

Row 18: *K1, p1, k14, p1, k1; repeat from * to end.

Repeat Rows 1 to 18.

CHART KEY:

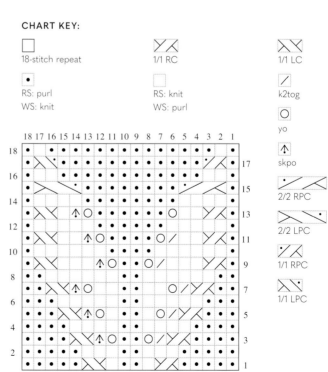

18-stitch repeat

1/1 RC

1/1 LC

RS: purl
WS: knit

RS: knit
WS: purl

k2tog

yo

skpo

2/2 RPC

2/2 LPC

1/1 RPC

1/1 LPC

Ironwork

This complex geometric panel is inspired by castle ironwork. Narrow cables mean that the fabric is softer and the cables appear to sit delicately on the surface of the reverse stockinette background.

Skill level:

SEC: 1 st should be added per 4in (10cm) finished width

Mix & match:
Stitches Multiple of 18 sts plus 4
Repeat 36-row pattern repeat plus 2 set-up rows

Row 1 (RS): K2, *k4, p4, k2, p4, k4; repeat from * to last 2 sts, k2.

Row 2 (WS): P2, *p4, k4, p2, k4, p4; repeat from * to last 2 sts, p2.

Row 3: K2, *k2, [1/1 RC, p4] twice, 1/1 RC, k2; repeat from * to last 2 sts, k2.

Row 4: Repeat Row 2.

Row 5: K2, *k1, 1/1 RPC, 1/1 LPC, p2, 1/1 RC, 1/1 LC, p2, 1/1 RPC, 1/1 LPC, k1; repeat from * to last 2 sts, k2.

Row 6: P2, *p2, k2, p1, k2, p4, k2, p1, k2, p2; repeat from * to last 2 sts, p2.

Row 7: 1/1 LPC, *1/1 RPC, p2, 1/1 LPC, 1/1 RC, k2, 1/1 LC, 1/1 RPC, p2, 1/1 LPC; repeat from * to last 2 sts, 1/1 RPC.

Row 8: K1, p1, *p1, k4, p8, k4, p1; repeat from * to last 2 sts, p1, k1.

Row 9: P1, *1/1 RC, p4, 1/1 LC, k4, 1/1 RC, p4; repeat from * to last 3 sts, 1/1 RC, p1.

Row 10: Repeat Row 8.

Row 11: P1, k1, *k1, p3, 1/1 RC, 1/1 LC, k2, 1/1 RC, 1/1 LC, p3, k1; repeat from * to last 2 sts, k1, p1.

Row 12: K1, p1, *p1, k3, p10, k3, p1; repeat from * to last 2 sts, p1, k1.

Row 13: P1, *1/1 RC, p2, [1/1 RC, k2, 1/1 LC] twice, p2; repeat from * to last 3 sts, 1/1 RC, p1.

Row 14: K1, p1, *p1, k2, p12, k2, p1; repeat from * to last 2 sts, p1, k1.

Row 15: P1, k1, *k1, p2, k5, 1/1 RC, k5, p2, k1; repeat from * to last 2 sts, k1, p1.

Row 16: Repeat Row 14.

Row 17: P1, *1/1 RC, p2, 1/1 LPC, k2, 1/1 RC, 1/1 LC, k2, 1/1 RPC, p2; repeat from * to last 3 sts, 1/1 RC, p1.

Row 18: Repeat Row 12.

Row 19: P1, k1, *k1, p3, 1/1 LPC, 1/1 RC, k2, 1/1 LC, 1/1 RPC, p3, k1; repeat from * to last 2 sts, k1, p1.

Row 20: Repeat Row 8.

Row 21: Repeat Row 9.

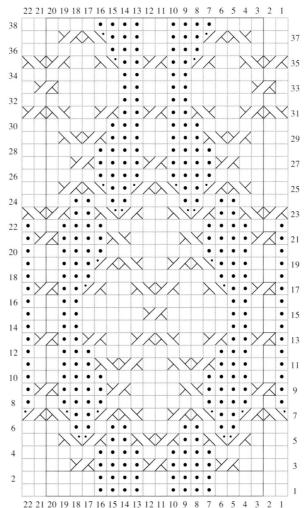

CHART KEY:

RS: knit
WS: purl

Set-up rows
(work once only)

RS: purl
WS: knit

18-stitch repeat

1/1 RC

1/1 RPC

1/1 LPC

1/1 LC

Row 22: Repeat Row 8.

Row 23: 1/1 RC, *1/1 LC, p2, 1/1 RPC, 1/1 LPC, k2, 1/1 RPC, 1/1 LPC, p2, 1/1 RC; repeat from * to last 2 sts, 1/1 LC.

Row 24: Repeat Row 6.

Row 25: K2, *k1, 1/1 LC, [1/1 RPC, p2, 1/1 LPC] twice, 1/1 RC, k1; repeat from * to last 2 sts, k2.

Row 26: Repeat Row 2.

Row 27: Repeat Row 3.

Row 28: Repeat Row 2.

Row 29: K2, *k1, 1/1 RC, 1/1 LC, p3, k2, p3, 1/1 RC, 1/1 LC, k1; repeat from * to last 2 sts, k2.

Row 30: P2, *p5, k3, p2, k3, p5; repeat from * to last 2 sts, p2.

Row 31: 1/1 LC, *1/1 RC, k2, 1/1 LC, [p2, 1/1 RC] twice, k2, 1/1 LC; repeat from * to last 2 sts, 1/1 RC.

Row 32: P2, *p6, k2, p2, k2, p6; repeat from * to last 2 sts, p2.

Row 33: K1, *1/1 RC, k5, p2, k2, p2, k5; repeat from * to last 3 sts, 1/1 RC, k1.

Row 34: Repeat Row 32.

Row 35: 1/1 RC, *1/1 LC, k2, 1/1 RPC, p2, 1/1 RC, p2, 1/1 LPC, k2, 1/1 RC; repeat from * to last 2 sts, 1/1 LC.

Row 36: Repeat Row 30.

Row 37: K2, *k1, 1/1 LC, 1/1 RPC, p3, k2, p3, 1/1 LPC, 1/1 RC, k1; repeat from * to last 2 sts, k2.

Row 38: Repeat Row 2.

Repeat Rows 3 to 38.

SEC: 18 sts should be added per 4in (10cm) finished width

Mix & match:
Stitches Multiple of 16 sts plus 4
Repeat 16-row pattern repeat

Reversible Twin Rib Garter

It's always handy to have reversible cables in your repertoire, and this stitch is a great choice. Use for scarves and other projects where both sides of the fabric will be on view.

Row 1 (RS): *K5, [p1, k1] 5 times, p1; repeat from * to last 4 sts, k4.

Row 2 and all WS rows: K4, *[k1, p1] 6 times, k4; repeat from * to end.

Row 3: Repeat Row 1.

Row 5: Repeat Row 1.

Row 7: Repeat Row 1.

Row 9: *K4, 2/2 RCL, [k1, p1] 4 times; repeat from * to last 4 sts, k4.

Row 11: Repeat Row 1.

Row 13: *K5, p1, k1, p1, 4/4 RCR; repeat from * to last 4 sts, k4.

Row 15: Repeat Row 9.

Row 16: Repeat Row 2.

Repeat Rows 1 to 16.

Special stitches

2/2 RCL: Slip next stitch to cable needle and place at front of work, [k1, p1] twice from cable needle.

4/4 RCR: Slip next 4 stitches to cable needle and hold to back of work. K1, p1, k1, p1. K1, p1, k1, p1 from cable needle.

CHART KEY:

☐ 16-stitch repeat	• RS: purl / WS: knit	⟋ 4/4 RCR
☐ RS: knit / WS: purl	⟍ 2/2 RCL	

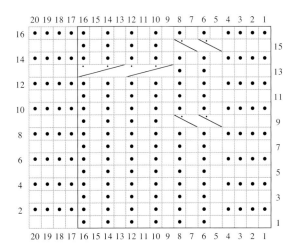

Skill level:

SEC: 14 sts should be added per 4in (10cm) finished width

Mix & match:
Stitches Multiple of 16 sts plus 4
Repeat 16-row pattern repeat plus 4 set-up rows

Reversible Rib and Seed Cable

Careful placement of knits and purls are used here to create a striking reversible cable. Ribbed cables and seed (moss) stitch are dramatic and look equally effective on both sides of the fabric.

Row 1 (RS): *[K1, p1] 8 times; repeat from * to last 4 sts, [k1, p1] twice.

Row 2 (WS): [P1, k1] twice, *[k1, p1] 5 times, k1, p2, k1, p1, k1; repeat from * to end.

Rows 3 and 4: Repeat Rows 1 and 2.

Row 5: *[K1, p1] 8 times; repeat from * to last 4 sts, [k1, p1] twice.

Row 6: [P1, k1] twice, *[k1, p1] 5 times, k1, p2, k1, p1, k1; repeat from * to end.

Rows 7 and 8: Repeat Rows 5 and 6.

Row 9: *[K1, p1] twice, 6/6 RCL; repeat from * to last 4 sts, [k1, p1] twice.

Row 10: Repeat Row 6.

Row 11: Repeat Row 5.

Rows 12 and 13: Repeat Rows 10 and 11.

Row 14: Repeat Row 6.

Row 15: *[K1, p1] 4 times, 2/2 RCL, [k1, p1] twice; repeat from * to last 4 sts, [k1, p1] twice.

Rows 16 and 17: Repeat Rows 14 and 15.

Row 18: [P1, k1] twice, *[k1, p1] 8 times; repeat from * to end.

Row 19: Repeat Row 15.

Row 20: Repeat Row 18.

Repeat Rows 5 to 18.

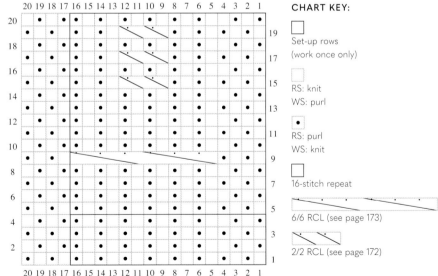

CHART KEY:

☐ Set-up rows (work once only)

☐ RS: knit
WS: purl

• RS: purl
WS: knit

☐ 16-stitch repeat

6/6 RCL (see page 173)

2/2 RCL (see page 172)

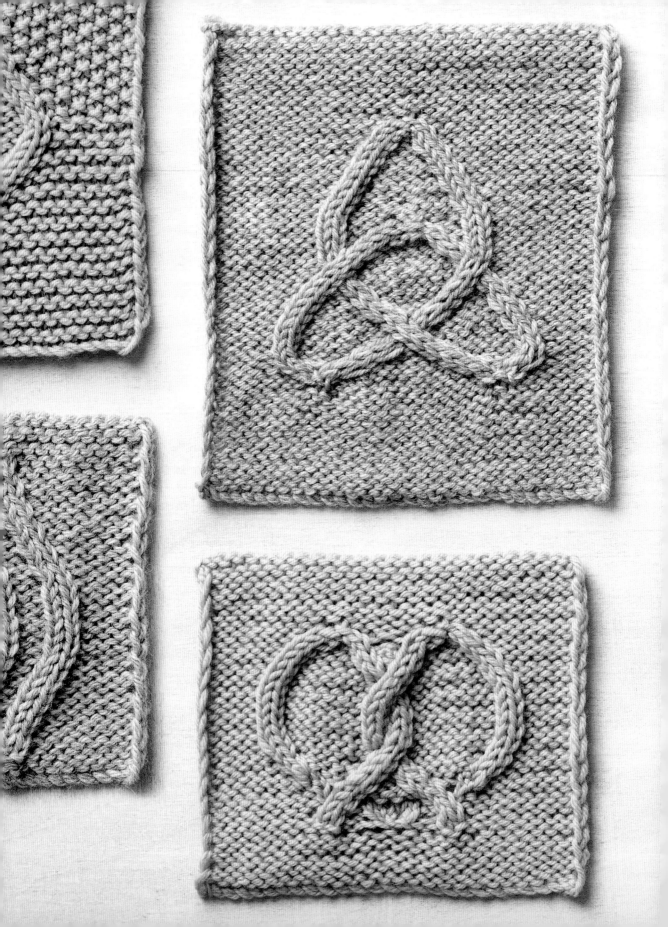

CHAPTER FIVE

Motifs and Panels

This chapter focuses on statement cables that really make an impact as single motifs and panels. We explore the "infinity circle" and cable square techniques, which allow you to create designs that can "float" as standalone features in the center of a piece.

Intersecting Ovals

This pattern has a very fluid, rhythmical feel. It looks beautiful as a standalone motif or work two or more repeats to add extra height and interest in a larger piece.

Skill level:

SEC: 6 sts should be added per 4in (10cm) finished width

Mix & match:
Stitches 28 sts
Repeat 28-row pattern repeat

Row 1 (RS): P6, [k4, p2] twice, k4, p6.

Row 2 (WS): K6, [p4, k2] twice, p4, k6.

Row 3: P5, [2/1 RPC, 2/1 LPC] 3 times, p5.

Row 4: K5, p2,[k2, p4] twice, k2, p2, k5.

Row 5: P4, 2/1 RPC, [p2, 2/2 RC] twice, p2, 2/1 LPC, p4.

Row 6: K4, p2, k3, p4, k2, p4, k3, p2, k4.

Row 7: P3, 2/1 RPC, p2, [2/1 RPC, 2/1 LPC] twice, p2, 2/1 LPC, p3.

Row 8: [K3, p2] twice, k2, p4, k2, [p2, k3] twice.

Row 9: [P2, 2/1 RPC] twice, p2, 2/2 LC, [p2, 2/1 LPC]twice, p2.

Row 10: K2, [p2, k3] twice, p4, k4, p1, k3, p2, k2.

Row 11: P1, [2/1 RPC, p2] twice, 2/1 RPC, [2/1 LPC, p2] twice, 2/1 LPC, p1.

Row 12: K1, [p2, k3] twice, p2, k2, [p2, k3] twice, p2, k1.

Row 13: P1, [k2, p3] twice, k2, p2, [k2, p3] twice, k2, p1.

Rows 14 to 17: Repeat Rows 12 and 13.

Row 18: Repeat Row 12.

Row 19: P1, [2/1 LPC, p2] twice, 2/1 LPC, [2/1 RPC, p2] twice, 2/1 RPC, p1.

Row 20: K2, [p2, k3] twice, p4, [k3, p2] twice, k2.

Row 21: [P2, 2/1 LPC] twice, p2, 2/2 LC, [p2, 2/1 RPC] twice, p2.

Row 22: Repeat Row 8.

Row 23: P3, 2/1 LPC, p2, [2/1 LPC, 2/1 RPC] twice, p2, 2/1 RPC, p3.

Row 24: Repeat Row 6.

Row 25: P4, 2/1 LPC, [p2, 2/2 RC] twice, p2, 2/1 RPC, p4.

Row 26: Repeat Row 4.

Row 27: P5, [2/1 LPC, 2/1 RPC] 3 times, p5.

Row 28: Repeat Row 2.

CHART KEY:

• RS: purl / WS: knit	☐ RS: knit / WS: purl	2/1 RPC	2/2 RC
		2/1 LPC	2/2 LC

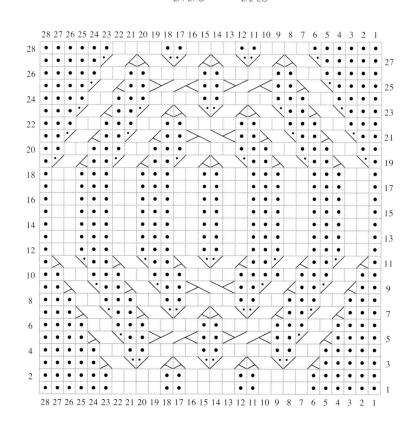

Garter and Seed Diamond Twist

Cable motifs can look equally dramatic when set against a textured background. This harlequin combination of seed (moss) and garter stitch really makes the central diamond pop.

Skill level:

SEC: 3 sts should be added per 4in (10cm) finished width

Mix & match:
Stitches 21 sts with variable stitch count
Repeat 38-row pattern repeat

Row 1 (RS): P10, k2, [p1, k1] 4 times, p1. (21 sts)

Row 2 (WS): [P1, k1] 5 times, p11.

Row 3: P10, m1, inc1to3, m1, [k1, p1] 5 times. (25 sts)

Row 4: [P1, k1] 5 times, p15.

Row 5: P8, 2/2 RC, k1, 2/2 LC, [k1, p1] 4 times.

Row 6: [P1, k1] 4 times, p17.

Row 7: P6, 2/2 RPC, 3/2 RC, 2/2 LPC, [k1, p1] 3 times.

Row 8: [P1, k1] 3 times, p2, k2, p5, k2, p8.

Row 9: P5, 2/1 RPC, p2, k5, p2, 2/1 LPC, [p1, k1] twice, p1.

Row 10: [P1, k1] twice, p3, k3, p5, k3, p7.

Row 11: P4, 2/1 RPC, p3, 3/2 RC, p3, 2/1 LPC, [k1, p1] twice.

Row 12: [P1, k1] twice, p2, k4, p5, k4, p6.

Row 13: P3, 2/1 RPC, p4, k5, p4, 2/1 LPC, p1, k1, p1.

Row 14: P1, k1, p3, [k5, p5] twice.

Row 15: P2, 2/1 RPC, p5, 3/2 RC, p5, 2/1 LPC, k1, p1.

Row 16: P1, k1, p2, k6, p5, k6, p4.

Row 17: P1, 2/1 RPC, p6, k5, p6, 2/1 LPC, p1.

Row 18: P3, k7, p5, k7, p3.

Row 19: 2/1 RPC, p7, 3/2 RC, p7, 2/1 LPC.

Row 20: P2, k8, p5, k8, p2.

Row 21: 2/1 LC, p7, k5, p7, 2/1 RC.

Row 22: K1, p2, k7, p5, k7, p2, k1.

Row 23: K1, 2/1 LPC, p6, 3/2 RC, p6, 2/1 RC, k1.

Row 24: K2, p2, k6, p5, k6, p3, k1.

Row 25: K1, p1, 2/1 LC, p5, k5, p5, 2/1 RC, k2.

Row 26: K3, p2, k5, p5, k5, p2, k1, p1, k1.

Row 27: K1, p1, k1, 2/1 LPC, p4, 3/2 RC, p4, 2/1 RC, k3.

Row 28: K4, p2, k4, p5, k4, p3, k1, p1, k1.

Row 29: [K1, p1] twice, 2/1 LC, p3, k5, p3, 2/1 RC, k4.

Row 30: K5, p2, k3, p5, k3, p2, [k1, p1] twice, k1.

Row 31: [K1, p1] twice, k1, 2/1 LPC, p2, 3/2 RC, p2, 2/1 RC, k5.

Row 32: K6, p2, k2, p5, k2, p3, [k1, p1] twice, k1.

Row 33: [K1, p1] 3 times, 2/2 LC, k5, 2/2 RC, k6.

Row 34: K8, p10, [k1, p1] 3 times, k1.

Row 35: [K1, p1] 4 times, 2/2 LC, k1, 2/2 RC, k8.

Row 36: K10, dec5to1, [k1, p1] 5 times. (21 sts)

Row 37: [K1, p1] 5 times, k11.

Row 38: K10, p2, [k1, p1] 4 times, k1.

CHART KEY:

- • RS: purl / WS: knit
- ▨ No stitch
- ☐ RS: knit / WS: purl
- ⟲ RS: m1 / WS: m1 purlwise
- inc1to3
- 2/2 RC
- 2/2 LC
- 2/2 RPC
- 3/2 RC
- 2/2 LPC
- 2/1 RPC
- 2/1 LPC
- 2/1 LC
- 2/1 RC
- Ⓐ dec5to1

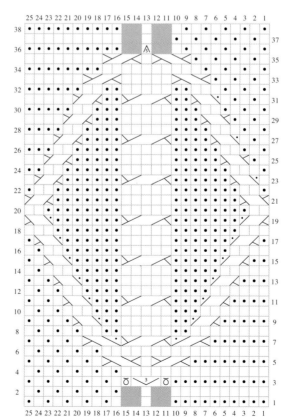

Triquetra

A very familiar celtic symbol, the trinity, triquetra, or triple moon is rich in meaning. Symbolizing the circle of life and death, mind, body, and spirit, it can be found in many places and cultures.

Skill level:

SEC: 2 sts should be added per 4in (10cm) finished width

Mix & match:
Stitches 21 sts with variable stitch count
Repeat 32-row pattern repeat

Row 1 (RS): Purl. (21 sts)

Row 2 (WS): Knit.

Row 3: P3, m1, inc1to3, m1, p13, m1, inc1to3, m1, p3. (29 sts)

Row 4: K3, p2, k1, p2, k13, p2, k1, p2, k3.

Row 5: P6, 2/3 LPC, p7, 2/3 RPC, p1, 2/3 LPC.

Row 6: [P2, k7] 3 times, p2.

Row 7: 2/1 LPC, p6, 2/3 LPC, p1, 2/3 RPC, p6, 2/1 RPC.

Row 8: [K1, p2, k9, p2] twice, k1.

Row 9: P1, 2/1 LPC, p8, 2/1/2 LC, p8, 2/1 RPC, p1.

Row 10: K2, p2, k8, p2, k1, p2, k8, p2, k2.

Row 11: P2, 2/1 LPC, p4, 2/3 RPC, p1, 2/3 LPC, p4, 2/1 RPC, p2.

Row 12: K3, p2, k4, p2, k7, p2, k4, p2, k3.

Row 13: P3, 2/2 LPC, 2/2 RPC, p7, 2/2 LPC, 2/2 RPC, p3.

Row 14: K5, p4, k11, p4, k5.

Row 15: P5, 2/2 RC, p11, 2/2 RC, p5.

Row 16: Repeat Row 14.

Row 17: P5, k2, 2/2 LPC, p6, 2/3 RPC, k2, p5.

Row 18: K5, p2, k3, p2, k6, p2, k2, p2, k5.

Row 19: P5, k2, p2, 2/3 LPC, p1, 2/2 RPC, p3, k2, p5.

Row 20: K5, p2, k5, dec5to1, k5, p2, k5. (25 sts)

Row 21: P5, 2/1 LPC, p9, 2/1 RPC, p5.

Row 22: K6, p2, k9, p2, k6.

Row 23: P6, 2/1 LPC, p7, 2/1 RPC, p6.

Row 24: [K7, p2] twice, k7.

Row 25: P7, 2/1 LPC, p5, 2/1 RPC, p7.

Row 26: K8, p2, k5, p2, k8.

Row 27: P8, 2/1 LPC, p3, 2/1 RPC, p8.

Row 28: K9, p2, k3, p2, k9.

Row 29: P9, 2/1 LPC, p1, 2/1 RPC, p9.

Row 30: K10, dec5to1, k10. (21sts)

Row 31: Purl.

Row 32: Knit.

CHART KEY:

- •
  RS: purl
  WS: knit

- ▨ No stitch

- ඊ
  RS: m1
  WS: m1 purlwise

- ⌣³ inc1to3

- ☐
  RS: knit
  WS: purl

- ⟋ 2/3 LPC

- ⟋ 2/3 RPC

- ⟍ 2/1 LPC

- ⟍ 2/1 RPC

- ⨉ 2/1/2 LC

- ⟍ 2/2 LPC

- ⟋ 2/2 RPC

- ⨉ 2/2 RC

- Ⓐ dec5to1

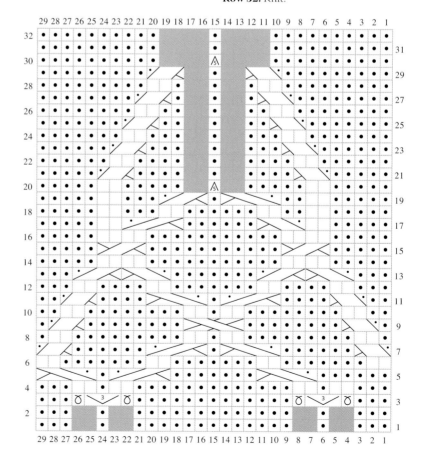

CHAPTER SIX

Cable Borders and Edges

Swap out or adapt traditional ribs for exciting cables and twists. Create edgings that become an integral part of your designs, harmonizing with the body of the piece or adding dramatic impact.

Skill level:

SEC: 10 sts should be added per 4in (10cm) finished width

Mix & match:
Stitches Multiple of 14 sts
Repeat 2-row pattern repeat

Narrow Twists—Right Edge

Simple but elegant, this edge makes an interesting alternative to a standard ribbed edge.

Row 1 (RS): *K2, 1/1 LC, p2, 1/1 RC, p2, k2, p2; repeat from * to end.
Row 2 (WS): *[K2, p2] twice, k2, p4; repeat from * to end.
Repeat Rows 1 and 2.

PATTERN TIPS
Change up the look by adding extra resting (plain) rows between the cables. Just remember to change both edges to make them match!

CHART KEY:

☐	⤬⤬ 1/1 LC	⤬⤬ 1/1 RC
14-stitch repeat		

☐ RS: knit / WS: purl	• RS: purl / WS: knit

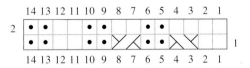

Skill level:

SEC: 10 sts should be added per 4in (10cm) finished width

Mix & match:
Stitches Multiple of 14 sts
Repeat 2-row pattern repeat

Narrow Twists—Left Edge

This is the left-hand edge of the same pattern on the opposite page.

Row 1 (RS): *P2, k2, p2, 1/1 LC, p2, 1/1 RC, k2; repeat from * to end.

Row 2 (WS): *P4, [k2, p2] twice, k2; repeat from * to end.

Repeat Rows 1 and 2.

PATTERN TIPS
Blend in the cable for a softer look by swapping the two knit stitches (Rows 3 and 4 on the left edge, and 11 and 12 on the corresponding right edge) for purl stitches on the RS, knit stitches on the WS.

CHART KEY:

☐ 14-stitch repeat	☐ RS: knit WS: purl	�><◁ 1/1 RC
• RS: purl WS: knit	◇◁ 1/1 LC	

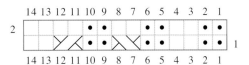

14 13 12 11 10 9 8 7 6 5 4 3 2 1

14 13 12 11 10 9 8 7 6 5 4 3 2 1

Saxon Braid

A classic, beautiful braid that creates a striking edging without adding too much weight.

Row 1 (RS): *P2, [k4, p4] twice, k4, p2; repeat from * to end.

Row 2 (WS): *K2, [p4, k4] twice, p4, k2; repeat from * to end.

Row 3: *P2, [2/2 RC, p4] twice, 2/2 RC, p2; repeat from * to end.

Row 4: Repeat Row 2.

Row 5: *P1, 2/1 RPC, [2/2 LPC, 2/2 RPC] twice, 2/1 LPC, p1; repeat from * to end.

Row 6: *K1, p2, k3, p4, k4, p4, k3, p2, k1; repeat from * to end.

Row 7: *2/1 RPC, p3, 2/2 LC, p4, 2/2 LC, p3, 2/1 LPC; repeat from * to end.

Row 8: Repeat Row 1.

Row 9: *K2, p2, [2/2 RPC, 2/2 LPC] twice, p2, k2; repeat from * to end.

Row 10: *P2, k2, p2, k4, p4, k4, p2, k2, p2; repeat from * to end.

Row 11: *K2, p2, k2, p4, 2/2 RC, p4, k2, p2, k2; repeat from * to end.

Row 12: Repeat Row 10.

Row 13: *K2, p2, [2/2 LPC, 2/2 RPC] twice, p2, k2; repeat from * to end.

Row 14: Repeat Row 1.

Row 15: *2/1 LPC, p3, 2/2 LC, p4, 2/2 LC, p3, 2/1 RPC; repeat from * to end.

Row 16: Repeat Row 6.

Row 17: *P1, 2/1 LPC, [2/2 RPC, 2/2 LPC] twice, 2/1 RPC, p1; repeat from * to end.

Row 18: Repeat Row 2.

Repeat Rows 3 to 18.

PATTERN NOTES
This pattern is the same whether made for a left-hand or right-hand edge.

CHART KEY:

☐ Set-up rows (work once only)

• RS: purl WS: knit

☐ RS: knit WS: purl

☐ 24-stitch repeat

2/2 RC

2/1 RPC

2/2 LPC

2/2 RPC

2/1 LPC

2/2 LC

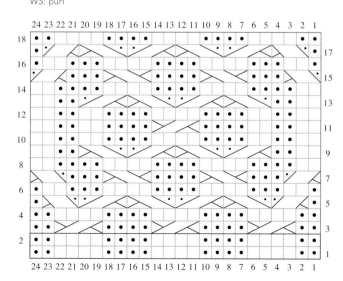

SEC: 4 sts should be added per 4in (10cm) finished width

Mix & match:
Stitches Multiple of 11 sts plus 4 (with variable stitch count)
Repeat 6-row pattern repeat

PATTERN NOTES
This pattern is the same whether made for a left-hand or right-hand edge.

Leafy Cable Rib

Set against a garter stitch background, this richly textured stitch could be used to great effect as an alternative to a standard rib.

Row 1 (RS): *K11; repeat from * to last 4 sts, k4.

Row 2 (WS): K4, *p7, k4; repeat from * to end.

Row 3: *K6, (k1, yo, k1) in 1 st, sl1, (k1, yo, k1) in 1 st, k2; repeat from * to last 4 sts, k4. (4 sts inc per repeat)

Row 4: K4, *p2, slwyif 3 times, k1, slwyif 3 times, p2, k4; repeat from * to end.

Row 5: *K4, 2/3 K3togR, sl1, 2/3 K3togL.; repeat from * to last 4 sts, k4.

Row 6: Repeat Row 2. (15 sts)

Repeat Rows 1 to 6.

Special stitch

slwyif: Slip 1 stitch purlwise with yarn in front.

2/3 K3togR: Slip next 2 sts to cable needle and place at back of work. Knit next 3 sts together through back of loop (decreasing 2 sts), k2 from cable needle.

2/3 K3togL: Slip next 2 sts to cable needle and place at front of work. Knit next 3 sts together through back of loop (decreasing 2 sts), k2 from cable needle.

CHART KEY:

☐ 11-stitch repeat

☐ RS: knit
WS: purl

▨ No stitch

• RS: purl
WS: knit

⌄ RS: (k1, yo, k1) in 1 stitch

V RS: slip
WS: slwyif

◿ 2/3 K3togR

◺ 2/3 K3togL

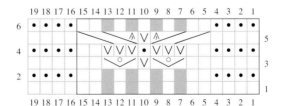

SEC: 3 sts should be added per 4in (10cm) finished width

Mix & match:
Stitches Multiple of 11 sts with variable stitch count
Repeat 24-row pattern repeat plus 4 set-up rows

PATTERN NOTES
For a left-hand edge, when working Row 27 simply replace the 2/1/2 LPC with 2/1/2 RPC.

Circles and Crosses

Bold and dramatic, this edging would look particularly good when worked in a bulky (chunky) yarn.

Row 1 (RS): *P3, k2, p1, k2, p3; repeat from * to end. (11 sts)

Row 2 (WS): *K3, p2, k1, p2, k3; repeat from * to end.

Row 3: Repeat Row 1.

Row 4: Repeat Row 2.

Row 5: *P2, 2/1 RPC, p1, 2/1 LPC, p2; repeat from * to end.

Row 6: *K2, p2, k3, p2, k2; repeat from * to end.

Row 7: *P1, 2/1 RPC, p3, 2/1 LPC, p1; repeat from * to end.

Row 8: *K1, p2, k5, p2, k1; repeat from * to end.

Row 9: *2/1 RPC, p2, m1, inc1to3, m1, p2, 2/1 LPC; repeat from * to end. (4 sts inc per repeat)

Row 10: *P2, k3, p1 tbl, p1, k1, p1, p1 tbl, k3, p2; repeat from * to end.

Row 11: *2/1 LPC, 2/2 RPC, p1, 2/2 LPC, 2/1 RPC; repeat from * to end.

Row 12: *K1, p4, k5, p4, k1; repeat from * to end.

Row 13: *P1, 2/2 RPC, p5, 2/2 LPC, p1; repeat from * to end.

Row 14: *K1, p2, k9, p2, k1; repeat from * to end.

Row 15: *P1, k2, p9, k2, p1; repeat from * to end.

Row 16: Repeat Row 14.

Row 17: *P1, 2/2 LC, p5, 2/2 RC, p1; repeat from * to end.

Row 18: Repeat Row 12.

Row 19: *2/1 RPC, 2/2 LPC, p1, 2/2 RPC, 2/1 LPC; repeat from * to end.

Row 20: *P2, k3, p2, dec5to1, p2, k3, p2; repeat from * to end. (11 sts per repeat)

Row 21: *2/1 LPC, p2, p1 tbl, p2, 2/1 RPC; repeat from * to end.

Row 22: Repeat Row 8.

Row 23: *P1, 2/1 LPC, p3, 2/1 RPC, p1; repeat from * to end.

Row 24: Repeat Row 6.

Row 25: *P2, 2/1 LPC, p1, 2/1 RPC, p2; repeat from * to end.

Row 26: Repeat Row 2.

Row 27: *P3, 2/1/2 LPC, p3; repeat from * to end.

Row 28: Repeat Row 2.

Repeat Rows 5 to 28.

CHART KEY:

☐ Set-up rows (work once only)

• RS: purl WS: knit

☐ RS: knit WS: purl

▨ No stitch

☐ 11-stitch repeat with variable stitch count

⟋⟍ 2/1 RPC

⟍⟋ 2/1 LPC

Ⓞ RS: m1 WS: m1 purlwise

⟍3⟋ inc1to3

Ⓠ RS: k tbl WS: p tbl

⟍⟋ 2/2 RPC

⟋⟍ 2/2 LPC

⟩⟨ 2/2 LC

⟩⟨ 2/2 RC

Ⓐ dec5to1

Ⓠ RS: p tbl WS: k tbl

⟩⟨ 2/1/2 LPC

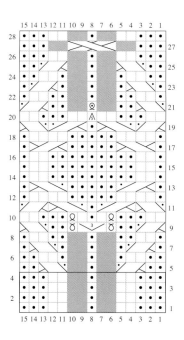

Skill level:

SEC: 1 st should be deducted per 4in (10cm) finished width

Mix & match:
Stitches Multiple of 5 sts plus 3
Repeat 8-row pattern repeat

Asymmetric Twisted Rib

A simple but effective cable. Very useful for adding a little extra interest to a design and can be readily adapted to both horizontal and vertical edges.

Row 1 (RS): *P1, k1, p1, k2; repeat from * to last 3 sts, p1, k1, p1.

Row 2 and all WS rows: K1, p1, k1, *p2, k1, p1, k1; repeat from * to end.

Row 3: *P1, k1, p1, 1/1 LC; repeat from * to last 3 sts, p1, k1, p1.

Row 5: Repeat Row 1.

Row 7: Repeat Row 3.

Row 8: K1, p1, k1, *p2, k1, p1, k1; repeat from * to end.

Repeat Rows 1 to 8.

PATTERN NOTES
1/1 LC in Rows 3 and 7 should be replaced with 1/1 RC for a left-hand edge.

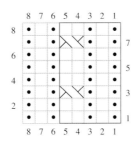

CHART KEY:

5-stitch repeat

RS: purl
WS: knit

RS: knit
WS: purl

1/1 LC

Skill level:

SEC: 0 sts should be added per 4in (10cm) finished width

Mix & match:
Stitches Multiple of 11 sts with variable stitch count
Repeat 36-row pattern repeat plus 2 set-up rows

Hourglass Seeded Twist—Right Edge

This bold edging could be worked either across a horizontal or vertical edge. Add stitches around the repeat to create different looks.

Row 1 (RS): Purl. (11 sts)

Row 2 (WS): Knit.

Row 3: *P5, m1, inc1to3, m1, p5; repeat from * to end. (15 sts per repeat)

Row 4: *K5, p2, (p1, yo, p1) in 1 st, p2, k5; repeat from * to end. (17 sts per repeat)

Row 5: *P3, 3/2 RPC, k1, 3/2 LPC, p3; repeat from * to end.

Row 6: *K3, p3, [k1, p1] twice, k1, p3, k3; repeat from * to end.

Row 7: *P2, 3/1 RPC, [k1, p1] twice, k1, 3/1 LPC, p2; repeat from * to end.

Row 8: *K2, p4, [k1, p1] twice, k1, p4, k2; repeat from * to end.

Row 9: *P1, 3/1 RC, [p1, k1] 3 times, p1, 3/1 LC, p1; repeat from * to end.

Row 10: *K1, p3, [k1, p1] 4 times, k1, p3, k1; repeat from * to end.

Row 11: *P1, k4, [p1, k1] 3 times, p1, k4, p1; repeat from * to end.

Row 12: Repeat Row 10.

Row 13: *P1, 3/1 LPC, [p1, k1] 3 times, p1, 3/1 RPC, p1; repeat from * to end.

Row 14: Repeat Row 8.

Row 15: *P2, 3/1 LPC, [k1, p1] twice, k1, 3/1 RPC, p2; repeat from * to end.

Row 16: Repeat Row 6.

Row 17: *P3, 3/1 LPC, p1, k1, p1, 3/1 RPC, p3; repeat from * to end.

Row 18: *K4, p4, k1, p4, k4; repeat from * to end.

Row 19: *P4, 3/1 LPC, k1, 3/1 RPC, p4; repeat from * to end.

Row 20: *K5, p3, k1, p3, k5; repeat from * to end.

Row 21: *P5, 3/1/3 LPC, p5; rep from * to end.

Row 22: Repeat Row 20.

Row 23: *P4, 3/1 RPC, k1, 3/1 LPC, p4; repeat from * to end.

Row 24: Repeat Row 18.

Row 25: *P3, 3/1 RC, p1, k1, p1, 3/1 LC, p3; repeat from * to end.

Row 26: Repeat Row 6.

Row 27: Repeat Row 7.

Row 28: Repeat Row 8.

Row 29: Repeat Row 9.

Row 30: Repeat Row 10.

Row 31: Repeat Row 11.

Row 32: Repeat Row 10.

Row 33: Repeat Row 13.

Row 34: Repeat Row 8.

Row 35: Repeat Row 15.

Row 36: Repeat Row 6.

Row 37: *P3, 3/2 LPC, k1, 3/2 RPC, p3; repeat from * to end.

Row 38: *K5, dec7to1, k5; repeat from * to end. (11 sts per repeat)

Repeat Rows 3 to 38.

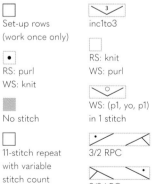

CHART KEY:

▢ Set-up rows (work once only)

• RS: purl
WS: knit

▨ No stitch

▢ 11-stitch repeat with variable stitch count

⊗ RS: m1
WS: m1 purlwise

◿ inc1to3

▢ RS: knit
WS: purl

◡ WS: (p1, yo, p1) in 1 stitch

3/2 RPC

3/2 LPC

3/1 RPC

3/1 LPC

3/1 RC

3/1 LC

3/1/3 LPC

Λ dec7to1

Skill level:

SEC: 0 sts should be added per 4in (10cm) finished width

Mix & match:
Stitches Multiple of 11 sts with variable stitch count
Repeat 36-row pattern repeat plus 2 set-up rows

Hourglass Seeded Twist—Left Edge

This is the left-hand edge of the pattern on the opposite page.

Row 1 (RS): Purl. (11 sts)

Row 2 (WS): Knit.

Row 3: *P5, m1, inc1to3, m1, p5; repeat from * to end. (15 sts per repeat)

Row 4: *K5, p2, (p1, yo, p1) in 1 st, p2, k5; repeat from * to end. (17 sts per repeat)

Row 5: *P3, 3/2 RPC, k1, 3/2 LPC, p3; repeat from * to end.

Row 6: *K3, p3, [k1, p1] twice, k1, p3, k3; repeat from * to end.

Row 7: *P2, 3/1 RPC, [k1, p1] twice, k1, 3/1 LPC, p2; repeat from * to end.

Row 8: *K2, p4, [k1, p1] twice, k1, p4, k2; repeat from * to end.

Row 9: *P1, 3/1 RC, [p1, k1] 3 times, p1, 3/1 LC, p1; repeat from * to end.

Row 10: *K1, p3, [k1, p1] 4 times, k1, p3, k1; repeat from * to end.

Row 11: *P1, k4, [p1, k1] 3 times, p1, k4, p1; repeat from * to end.

Row 12: Repeat Row 10.

Row 13: *P1, 3/1 LPC, [p1, k1] 3 times, p1, 3/1 RPC, p1; repeat from * to end.

Row 14: Repeat Row 8.

Row 15: *P2, 3/1 LPC, [k1, p1] twice, k1, 3/1 RPC, p2; repeat from * to end.

Row 16: Repeat Row 6.

Row 17: *P3, 3/1 LPC, p1, k1, p1, 3/1 RPC, p3; repeat from * to end.

Row 18: *K4, p4, k1, p4, k4; repeat from * to end.

Row 19: *P4, 3/1 LPC, k1, 3/1 RPC, p4; repeat from * to end.

Row 20: *K5, p3, k1, p3, k5; repeat from * to end.

Row 21: *P5, 3/1/3 RPC, p5; repeat from * to end.

Row 22: Repeat Row 20.

Row 23: *P4, 3/1 RPC, k1, 3/1 LPC, p4; repeat from * to end.

Row 24: Repeat Row 18.

Row 25: *P3, 3/1 RC, p1, k1, p1, 3/1 LC, p3; repeat from * to end.

Row 26: Repeat Row 6.

Row 27: Repeat Row 7.

Row 28: Repeat Row 8.

Row 29: Repeat Row 9.

Row 30: Repeat Row 10.

Row 31: Repeat Row 11.

Row 32: Repeat Row 10.

Row 33: Repeat Row 13.

Row 34: Repeat Row 8.

Row 35: Repeat Row 15.

Row 36: Repeat Row 6.

Row 37: *P3, 3/2 LPC, k1, 3/2 RPC, p3; repeat from * to end.

Row 38: *K5, dec7to1, k5; repeat from * to end. (11 sts per repeat)

Repeat Rows 3 to 38.

CHART KEY:

Set-up rows (work once only)

•
RS: purl
WS: knit

No stitch

11-stitch repeat with variable stitch count

RS: m1
WS: m1 purlwise

inc1to3

RS: knit
WS: purl

WS: (p1, yo, p1) in 1 stitch

3/2 RPC

3/2 LPC

3/1 RPC

3/1 LPC

3/1 RC

3/1 LC

3/1/3 RPC

dec7to1

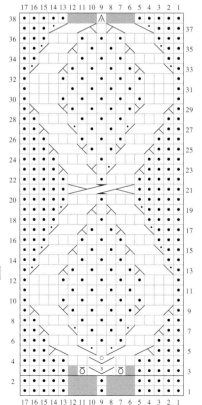

Skill level:

SEC: 12 sts should be added per 4in (10cm) finished width

Mix & match:
Stitches Multiple of 12 sts
Repeat 10-row pattern repeat plus 2 set-up rows

Swooping Curved Cable Left Twist—Right Edge

A combination of two cables creates a stable edging without being too stiff or inflexible.

Row 1 (RS): *P1, k2, p4, k4, p1; repeat from * to end.

Row 2 (WS): *K1, p4, k4, p2, k1; repeat from * to end.

Row 3: *P1, k2, p4, 2/2 LC, p1; repeat from * to end.

Row 4: Repeat Row 2.

Row 5: *P1, 2/2 LPC, p2, k4, p1; repeat from * to end.

Row 6: *K1, p4, k2, p2, k3; repeat from * to end.

Row 7: *P3, 2/2 LC twice, p1; repeat from * to end.

Row 8: *K1, p8, k3; repeat from * to end.

Row 9: *P1, 2/2 RPC, 2/2 LPC, k2, p1; repeat from * to end.

Row 10: Repeat Row 2.

Row 11: Repeat Row 3.

Row 12: Repeat Row 2.

Repeat Rows 3 to 12.

CHART KEY:

☐ Set-up rows (work once only)

☐ 12-stitch repeat

• RS: purl
WS: knit

☐ RS: knit
WS: purl

⟋⟍ 2/2 LC

⟋⟍• 2/2 LPC

•⟋⟍ 2/2 RPC

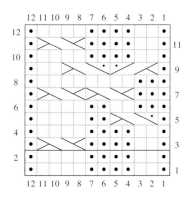

SEC: 12 sts should be added per 4in (10cm) finished width

Mix & match:
Stitches Multiple of 12 sts
Repeat 10-row pattern repeat plus 2 set-up rows

Swooping Curved Cable Right Twist–Left Edge

This is the left-hand edge of the same pattern on the opposite page.

Row 1 (RS): *P1, k4, p4, k2, p1; repeat from * to end. (12 sts)

Row 2 (WS): *K1, p2, k4, p4, k1; repeat from * to end.

Row 3: *P1, 2/2 RC, p4, k2, p1; repeat from * to end.

Row 4: Repeat Row 2.

Row 5: *P1, k4, p2, 2/2 RPC, p1; repeat from * to end.

Row 6: *K3, p2, k2, p4, k1; repeat from * to end.

Row 7: *P1, 2/2 RC twice, p3; repeat from * to end.

Row 8: *K3, p8, k1; repeat from * to end.

Row 9: *P1, k2, 2/2 RPC, 2/2 LPC, p1; repeat from * to end.

Row 10: Repeat Row 2.

Row 11: Repeat Row 3.

Row 12: Repeat Row 2.

Repeat Rows 3 to 12.

CHART KEY:

☐ Set-up rows (work once only)

• RS: purl
WS: knit

☐ RS: knit
WS: purl

☐ 12-stitch repeat

⤬ 2/2 RC

⤬ 2/2 RPC

⤬ 2/2 LPC

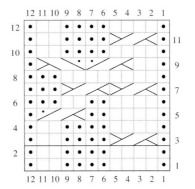

Skill level:

SEC: 2 sts should be deducted per 4in (10cm) finished width

Mix & match:
Stitches Multiple of 8 sts plus 3
Repeat 8-row pattern repeat

Cabled Rib—Right Edge

This delicate cable would look beautiful on any garment and is light enough to knit even in finer yarns.

Row 1 (RS): *P1, k1, p1, k5; repeat from * to last 3 sts, p1, k1, p1.

Row 2 and all WS rows: K1, p1, k1, *p5, k1, p1, k1; repeat from * to end.

Row 3: *[P1, k1] twice, 1/2 RC, k1; repeat from * to last 3 sts, p1, k1, p1.

Row 5: Repeat Row 1.

Row 7: *[P1, k1] twice, 1/2 LC, k1; repeat from * to last 3 sts, p1, k1, p1.

Row 8: K1, p1, k1, *p5, k1, p1, k1; repeat from * to end.

Repeat Rows 1 to 8.

CHART KEY:

☐ 8-stitch repeat	☐ RS: knit WS: purl	⧅ 1/2 LC
▪ RS: purl WS: knit		⧄ 1/2 RC

PATTERN TIPS

When pairing cables for edgings, be sure to line up the cables so that they mirror each other. In this case, Rows 3 and 7 should be the cable rows on both edges.

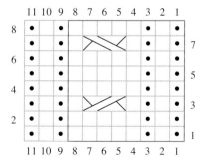

Skill level:

SEC: 2 sts should be deducted per 4in (10cm) finished width

Mix & match:
Stitches Multiple of 8 sts plus 3
Repeat 8-row pattern repeat

Cabled Rib—Left Edge

This is the left-hand edge of the same pattern on the opposite page..

Row 1 (RS): P1, k1, p1,*k5, p1, k1, p1; repeat from * to end. (11 sts)

Row 2 and all WS rows: *K1, p1, k1, p5; repeat to last 3 sts, k1, p1, k1.

Row 3: P1, k1, p1, *k1, 1/2 LC, [k1, p1] twice; repeat from * to end.

Row 5: Repeat Row 1.

Row 7: P1, k1, p1; *k1, 1/2 RC, [k1, p1] twice; repeat from * to end.

Row 8: *K1, p1, k1, p5; repeat from * to last 3 sts, k1, p1, k1.

Repeat Rows 1 to 8.

CHART KEY:

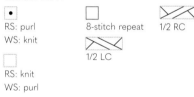

·
RS: purl
WS: knit

☐
8-stitch repeat

⬊ 1/2 RC

☐
RS: knit
WS: purl

⬈ 1/2 LC

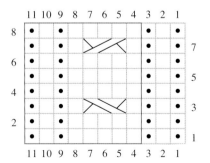

Skill level: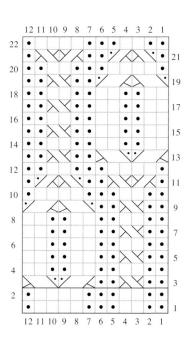

SEC: 2 sts should be added per 4in (10cm) finished width

Mix & match:
Stitches Multiple of 12 sts
Repeat 20-row pattern repeat plus 2 set-up rows

Twin Oval Twist—Right Edge

Two offset cables with extended ovals give an interesting edge without adding too much weight.

Row 1 (RS): *P2, k2, p3, k4, p1; repeat from *. (12 sts)

Row 2 (WS): *K1, p4, k3, p2, k2; repeat from * to end.

Row 3: *P2, 1/1 LC, p2, 2/1 RPC, 2/1 LPC; repeat from * to end.

Row 4: *[P2, k2] 3 times; repeat from * to end.

Row 5: *P2, 1/1 LC, [p2, k2] twice; repeat from * to end.

Rows 6 and 7: Repeat Rows 4 and 5.

Row 8: Repeat Row 4.

Row 9: *P2, 1/1 LC, p2, 2/1 LPC, 2/1 RPC; repeat from * to end.

Row 10: Repeat Row 2.

Row 11: *P1, 1/1 RC, 1/1 LC, p2, 1/1 LPC, 1/1 RPC, p1; repeat from * to end.

Row 12: *K2, p2, k3, p4, k1; repeat from * to end.

Row 13: *2/1 RPC, 2/1 LPC, p2, 1/1 LC, p2; repeat from * to end.

Row 14: *[K2, p2] 3 times; repeat from * to end.

Row 15: *[K2, p2] twice, 1/1 LC, p2; repeat from * to end.

Rows 16 and 17: Repeat Rows 14 and 15.

Row 18: Repeat Row 14.

Row 19: *2/1 LPC, 2/1 RPC, p2, 1/1 LC, p2; repeat from * to end.

Row 20: Repeat Row 12.

Row 21: *P1, 1/1 LPC, 1/1 RPC, p2, 1/1 RC, 1/1 LC, p1; repeat from * to end.

Row 22: Repeat Row 2.

Repeat Rows 3 to 22.

CHART KEY:

☐ Set-up rows (work once only)

⊡ RS: purl
WS: knit

☐ RS: knit
WS: purl

☐ 12-stitch repeat

⧄ 1/1 LC

⧄ 2/1 RPC

⧅ 2/1 LPC

⧄ 1/1 RC

⧄ 1/1 LPC

⧄ 1/1 RPC

Skill level:

SEC: 2 sts should be added per 4in (10cm) finished width

Mix & match:
Stitches Multiple of 12 sts
Repeat 20-row pattern repeat plus 2 set-up rows

Twin Oval Twist—Left Edge

This is the left-hand edge of the same pattern on the opposite page.

Row 1 (RS): *P1, k4, p3, k2, p2; repeat from * to end.

Row 2 (WS): *K2, p2, k3, p4, k1; repeat from * to end.

Row 3: *2/1 RPC, 2/1 LPC, p2, 1/1 RC, p2; repeat from * to end.

Row 4: *[K2, p2] 3 times; repeat from * to end.

Row 5: *[K2, p2] twice, 1/1 RC, p2; repeat from * to end.

Rows 6 and 7: Repeat Rows 4 and 5.

Row 8: Repeat Row 4.

Row 9: *2/1 LPC, 2/1 RPC, p2, 1/1 RC, p2; repeat from * to end.

Row 10: Repeat Row 2.

Row 11: *P1, 1/1 LPC, 1/1 RPC, p2, 1/1 RC, 1/1 LC, p1; repeat from * to end.

Row 12: *K1, p4, k3, p2, k2; repeat from * to end.

Row 13: *P2, 1/1 RC, p2, 2/1 RPC, 2/1 LPC; repeat from * to end.

Row 14: *[P2, k2] 3 times; repeat from * to end.

Row 15: *P2, 1/1 RC, [p2, k2] twice; repeat from * to end.

Rows 16 and 17: Repeat Rows 14 and 15.

Row 18: Repeat Row 14.

Row 19: *P2, 1/1 RC, p2, 2/1 LPC, 2/1 RPC; repeat from * to end.

Row 20: Repeat Row 12.

Row 21: *P1, 1/1 RC, 1/1 LC, p2, 1/1 LPC, 1/1 RPC, p1; repeat from * to end.

Row 22: Repeat Row 2.

Repeat Rows 3 to 22.

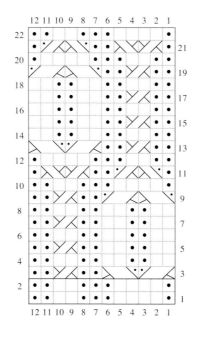

CHART KEY:

Set-up rows (work once only)

• RS: purl
WS: knit

RS: knit
WS: purl

12-stitch repeat

2/1 RPC

2/1 LPC

1/1 RC

1/1 LC

1/1 LPC

1/1 RPC

Skill level: ◐ ◐

SEC: 2 sts should be added per 4in (10cm) finished width

Mix & match:
Stitches Multiple of 6 sts plus 2
Repeat 8-row pattern repeat plus 2 set-up rows

Lacy Eights

Work this delicate, lacy cable as either a horizontal edging as shown, or take one or more repeats and work vertically—both will look equally pretty!

Row 1 (RS): *P2, k4; repeat from * to last 2 sts, p2.

Row 2 (WS): K2, *p4, k2; repeat from * to end.

Row 3: *P2, 2/2 LC; repeat from * to last 2 sts, p2.

Row 4: K2, *ssp, yo, p2, k2; repeat from * to end.

Row 5: *P2, k2tog, yo, k2; repeat from * to last 2 sts, p2.

Rows 6 to 7: Repeat Rows 4 and 5.

Row 8: Repeat Row 2.

Repeat Rows 3 to 8.

PATTERN NOTES
This pattern is the same whether made for a left-hand or right-hand edge.

CHART KEY:

▢ Set-up rows (work once only)

▢ 6-stitch repeat

◟ WS: ssp

• RS: purl
WS: knit

✕ 2/2 LC

◞ RS: k2tog

▢ RS: knit
WS: purl

O yo

SEC: 1 st should be added per 4in (10cm) finished width

Mix & match:
Stitches Multiple of 17 sts plus 3 (with variable stitch count)
Repeat 18-row pattern repeat

Infinity Circle and Rope Twist

Small cable circles with a twist between. This edging would work equally well as a horizontal or vertical edge by varying the spacing or location of the elements.

Row 1 (RS): Purl

Row 2 (WS): Knit.

Rows 3 and 4: Repeat Rows 1 and 2.

Row 5: P1, *p5, m1, inc1to3, m1, p11; repeat from * to last 2 sts, p2. (21 sts per pattern repeat plus 3 sts)

Row 6: K2, *k11, p2, k1, p2, k5; repeat from * to last st, k1.

Row 7: P1, *p3, 2/2 RPC, p1, 2/2 LPC, p9; repeat from * to last 2 sts, p2.

Row 8: K2, *k9, p2, k5, p2, k3; repeat from * to last st, k1.

Row 9: P1, *p1, 2/2 RPC, p1, 1/2 LC, p1, 2/2 LPC, p1, 1/2 LC, 1/2 RC; repeat from * to last 2 sts, p2.

Row 10: K2, *p6, k1, p2, k3, p3, k3, p2, k1; repeat from * to last st, k1.

Row 11: P1, *p1, k2, p3, 1/2 LC, p3, k2, p1, 1/2 LC, 1/2 RC; repeat from * to last 2 sts, p2.

Row 12: Repeat Row 10.

Row 13: P1, *p1, 2/2 LPC, p1, 1/2 LC, p1, 2/2 RPC, p1, 1/2 LC, 1/2 RC; repeat from * to last 2 sts, p2.

Row 14: Repeat Row 8.

Row 15: P1, *p3, 2/2 LPC, p1, 2/2 RPC, p9; repeat from * to last 2 sts, p2.

Row 16: K2, *k11, p2, dec5to1, p2, k5; repeat from * to last st, k1.

Row 17: Purl. (17 sts per pattern repeat plus 3 sts)

Row 18: Knit.

Repeat Rows 1 to 18.

PATTERN NOTES
This pattern is the same whether made for a left-hand or right-hand edge.

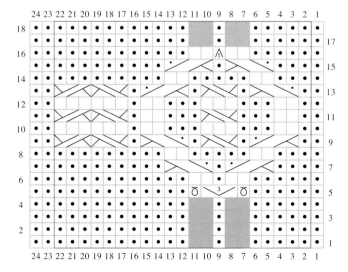

CHART KEY:

▢ 17-stitch repeat (variable stitch count)

• RS: purl / WS: knit

▨ No stitch

O̅ RS: m1

⌄‾3 inc1to3

▢ RS: knit / WS: purl

⟋⟍ 2/2 RPC

⟍⟋ 2/2 LPC

⟍⟋ 1/2 LC

⟍⟋ 1/2 RC

/Ⱥ\ dec5to1

Parallelogram Seed Stitch Cable— Right Edge

Skill level: ○ ○ ○

SEC: 1 st should be deducted per 4in (10cm) finished width

Mix & match:
Stitches Multiple of 17 sts plus 3
Repeat 30-row pattern repeat

A deep, richly-textured edging that would make a dramatic addition to projects knitted in heavier yarns where a bold border is required.

Row 1 (RS): *K5, [p1, k1] 4 times, p1, k3; repeat from * to last 3 sts, k3.

Row 2 (WS): K3, *p2, [k1, p1] 4 times, k1, p3, k3; repeat from * to end.

Row 3: *K5, [p1, k1] 4 times, 2/2 RC; repeat from * to last 3 sts, k3.

Row 4: K3, *p4, [k1, p1] 3 times, k1, p3, k3; repeat from * to end.

Row 5: *K5, [p1, k1] 3 times, 2/2 RPC, k2; repeat from * to last 3 sts, k3.

Row 6: K3, *p2, k2, p2, [k1, p1] twice, k1, p3, k3; repeat from * to end.

Row 7: *K5, [p1, k1] twice, 2/2 RPC, p2, k2; repeat from * to last 3 sts, k3.

Row 8: K3, *p2, k4, p2, k1, p1, k1, p3, k3; repeat from * to end.

Row 9: *K5, p1, k1, 2/2 RPC, p2, 2/2 RC; repeat from * to last 3 sts, k3.

Row 10: K3, *p4, k4, p2, k1, p3, k3; repeat from * to end.

Row 11: *K5, 2/2 RPC, p2, 2/2 RPC, k2; repeat from * to last 3 sts, k3.

Row 12: K3, *p2, k2, p2, k4, p4, k3; repeat from * to end.

Row 13: *K3, [2/2 RPC, p2] twice, k2; repeat from * to last 3 sts, k3.

Row 14: K3, *[p2, k4] twice, p2, k3; repeat from * to end.

Row 15: *K5, p2, 2/2 RPC, p2, 2/2 RC; repeat from * to last 3 sts, k3.

Row 16: K3, *p4, k4, p2, k2, p2, k3; repeat from * to end.

Row 17: *K5, 2/2 RPC, p2, 2/2 RC, k2; repeat from * to last 3 sts, k3.

Row 18: K3, *p2, k1, p3, k4, p4, k3; repeat from * to end.

Row 19: *K3, 2/2 RPC, p2, 2/2 RC, p1, k3; repeat from * to last 3 sts, k3.

Row 20: K3, *p2, k1, p1, k1, p3, k4, p2, k3; repeat from * to end.

Row 21: *K5, p2, 2/2 RC, p1, k1, p1, k3; repeat from * to last 3 sts, k3.

Row 22: K3, *p2, [k1, p1] twice, k1, p3, k2, p2, k3; repeat from * to end.

Row 23: *K5, 2/2 RC, [p1, k1] twice, p1, k3; repeat from * to last 3 sts, k3.

Row 24: K3, *p2, [k1, p1] 3 times, k1, p5, k3; repeat from * to end.

Row 25: *K3, 2/2 RC, [p1, k1] 3 times, p1, k3; repeat from * to last 3 sts, k3.

Row 26: Repeat Row 2.

Row 27: Repeat Row 1.

Rows 28 and 29: Repeat Rows 26 and 27.

Row 30: Repeat Row 2.

Repeat Rows 1 to 30.

CHART KEY:

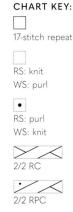

□ 17-stitch repeat

□ RS: knit
WS: purl

• RS: purl
WS: knit

⤬ 2/2 RC

⤬ 2/2 RPC

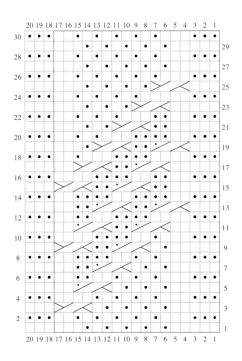

Parallelogram Seed Stitch Cable— Left Edge

This is the left-hand edge of the same pattern on the opposite page.

Skill level:

SEC: 1 st should be deducted per 4in (10cm) finished width

Mix & match:
Stitches Multiple of 13 sts
Repeat 30-row pattern repeat

Row 1 (RS): K3, *k3, [p1, k1] 4 times, p1, k5; repeat from * to end.

Row 2 (WS): *K3, p3, [k1, p1] 4 times, k1, p2; repeat from * to last 3 sts, k3.

Row 3: K3, *2/2 LC, [k1, p1] 4 times, k5; repeat from * to end.

Row 4: *K3, p3, [k1, p1] 3 times, k1, p4; repeat from * to last 3 sts, k3.

Row 5: K3, *k2, 2/2 LPC, [k1, p1] 3 times, k5; repeat from * to end.

Row 6: *K3, p3, [k1, p1] twice, k1, p2, k2, p2; repeat from * to last 3 sts, k3.

Row 7: K3, *k2, p2, 2/2 LPC, [k1, p1] twice, k5; repeat from * to end.

Row 8: K3, *p3, k1, p1, k1, p2, k4, p2; repeat from * to last 3 sts, k3.

Row 9: K3, *2/2 LC, p2, 2/2 LPC, k1, p1, k5; repeat from * to end.

Row 10: *K3, p3, k1, p2, k4, p4; repeat from * to last 3 sts, k3.

Row 11: K3, *k2, 2/2 LPC, p2, 2/2 LPC, k5; repeat from * to end.

Row 12: *K3, p4, k4, p2, k2, p2; repeat from * to last 3 sts, k3.

Row 13: K3, *k2, [p2, 2/2 LPC] twice, k3; repeat from * to end.

Row 14: *K3, [p2, k4] twice, p2; repeat from * to last 3 sts, k3.

Row 15: K3, *2/2 LC, p2, 2/2 LPC, p2, k5; repeat from * to end.

Row 16: *K3, p2, k2, p2, k4, p4; repeat from * to last 3 sts, k3.

Row 17: K3, *k2, 2/2 LC, p2, 2/2 LPC, k5.

Row 18: *K3, p4, k4, p3, k1, p2; repeat from * to last 3 sts, k3.

Row 19: K3, *k3, p1, 2/2 LC, p2, 2/2 LPC, k3; repeat from * to end.

Row 20: *K3, p2, k4, p3, k1, p1, k1, p2; repeat from * to last 3 sts, k3.

Row 21: K3, *k3, p1, k1, p1, 2/2 LC, p2, k5; repeat from * to end.

Row 22: *K3, p2, k2, p3, [k1, p1] twice, k1, p2; repeat from * to last 3 sts, k3.

Row 23: K3, *k3, [p1, k1] twice, p1, 2/2 LC, k5; repeat from * to end.

Row 24: *K3, p5, [k1, p1] 3 times, k1, p2; repeat from * to last 3 sts, k3.

Row 25: K3, *k3, [p1, k1] 3 times, p1, 2/2 LC, k3; repeat from * to end.

Row 26: Repeat Row 2.

Row 27: Repeat Row 1.

Rows 28 and 29: Repeat Rows 26 and 27.

Row 30: Repeat Row 2.

Repeat Rows 1 to 30.

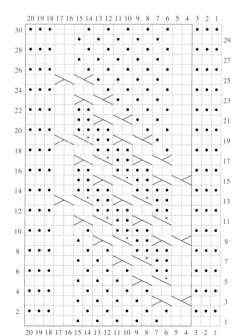

CHART KEY:

☐
RS: knit
WS: purl

☐
17-stitch repeat

•
RS: purl
WS: knit

⤫
2/2 LC

⤬
2/2 LPC

Skill level: ◐◐

SEC: 11 sts should be added per 4in (10cm) finished width

Mix & match:
Stitches Multiple of 10 sts plus 2
Repeat 36-row pattern repeat

Snaking Cable—Right Edge

A soft, curving cable that gives a lovely, fluid edging.

Row 1 (RS): *P2, k2, p4, k2; repeat from * to last 2 sts, p2.

Row 2 (WS): K2, *p2, k4, p2, k2; repeat from * to end.

Row 3: *P2, 2/2 LPC, 2/2 RPC; repeat from * to last 2 sts, p2.

Row 4: K2, *k2, p4, k4; repeat from * to end.

Row 5: *P4, 2/2 LPC, p2; repeat from * to last 2 sts, p2.

Row 6: K2, *k2, p2, k6; repeat from * to end.

Row 7: *P6, 2/1 LPC, p1; repeat from * to last 2 sts, p2.

Row 8: K2, *k1, p2, k7; repeat from * to end.

Row 9: *P7, 2/1 LPC; repeat from * to last 2 sts, p2.

Row 10: K2, *p2, k8; repeat from * to end.

Row 11: *P7, 2/1 RPC; repeat from * to last 2 sts, p2.

Row 12: Repeat Row 8.

Row 13: *P6, 2/1 RPC, p1; repeat from * to last 2 sts, p2.

Row 14: Repeat Row 6.

Row 15: *P4, 2/2 RC, p2; repeat from * to last 2 sts, p2.

Row 16: Repeat Row 4.

Row 17: *P2, 2/2 RPC, 2/2 LPC; repeat from * to last 2 sts, p2.

Row 18: Repeat Row 2.

Row 19: Repeat Row 1.

Row 20: Repeat Row 2.

Row 21: Repeat Row 3.

Row 22: Repeat Row 4.

Row 23: *P4, 2/2 RPC, p2; repeat from * to last 2 sts, p2.

Row 24: K2, *k4, p2, k4; repeat from * to end.

Row 25: *P3, 2/1 RPC, p4; repeat from * to last 2 sts, p2.

Row 26: K2, *k5, p2, k3; repeat from * to end.

Row 27: *P2, 2/1 RPC, p5; repeat from * to last 2 sts, p2.

Row 28: K2, *k6, p2, k2; repeat from * to end.

Row 29: *P2, 2/1 LPC, p5; repeat from * to last 2 sts, p2.

Row 30: Repeat Row 26.

Row 31: *P3, 2/1 LPC, p4; repeat from * to last 2 sts, p2.

Row 32: Repeat Row 24.

Row 33: *P4, 2/2 LC, p2; repeat from * to last 2 sts, p2.

Row 34: Repeat Row 4.

Row 35: Repeat Row 17.

Row 36: Repeat Row 2.

Repeat Rows 1 to 36.

CHART KEY:

☐ 10-stitch repeat

• RS: purl
WS: knit

☐ RS: knit
WS: purl

⟋ 2/2 LPC

⟋ 2/2 RPC

⟋ 2/1 LPC

⟋ 2/1 RPC

⟍ 2/2 RC

⟋ 2/2 LC

Skill level:

SEC: 11 sts should be added per 4in (10cm) finished width

Mix & match:
Stitches Multiple of 10 sts plus 2
Repeat 36-row pattern repeat

Snaking Cable—Left Edge

This is the left-hand edge of the same pattern on the opposite page.

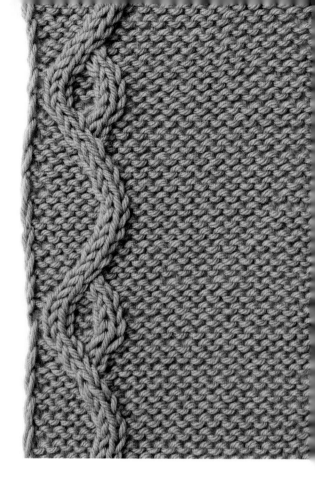

Row 1 (RS): P2, *k2, p4, k2, p2; repeat from * to end.

Row 2 (WS): *K2, p2, k4, p2; repeat from * to last 2 sts, k2.

Row 3: P2, *2/2 LPC , 2/2 RPC, p2; repeat from * to end.

Row 4: *K4, p4, k2; repeat from * to last 2 sts, k2.

Row 5: P2,*p2, 2/2 RPC, p4; repeat from * to end.

Row 6: *K6, p2, k2; repeat from * to last 2 sts, k2.

Row 7: P2, *p1, 2/1 RPC, p6; repeat from * to end.

Row 8: *K7, p2, k1; repeat from * to last 2 sts, k2.

Row 9: P2, *2/1 RPC, p7; repeat from * to end.

Row 10: K8, p2; repeat from * to last 2 sts, k2.

Row 11: P2, *2/1 LPC, p7; repeat from * to end.

Row 12: Repeat Row 8.

Row 13: P2, *p1, 2/1 LPC, p6; repeat from * to end.

Row 14: Repeat Row 6.

Row 15: P2, *p2, 2/2 LC, p4; repeat from * to end.

Row 16: Repeat Row 4.

Row 17: P2, *2/2 RPC, 2/2 LPC, p2; repeat from * to end.

Row 18: Repeat Row 2.

Row 19: Repeat Row 1.

Row 20: Repeat Row 2.

Row 21: Repeat Row 3.

Row 22: Repeat Row 4.

Row 23: P2, *p2, 2/2 LPC, p4; repeat from * to end.

Row 24: *K4, p2, k4; repeat from * to last 2 sts, k2.

Row 25: P2, *p4, 2/1 LPC, p3; repeat from * to end.

Row 26: *K3, p2, k5; repeat from * to last 2 sts, k2.

Row 27: P2, *p5, 2/1 LPC, p2; repeat from * to end.

Row 28: *K2, p2, k6; repeat from * to last 2 sts, k2.

Row 29: P2, *p5, 2/1 RPC, p2; repeat from * to end.

Row 30: Repeat Row 26.

Row 31: P2, *p4, 2/1 RPC, p3; repeat from * to end.

Row 32: Repeat Row 24.

Row 33: P2, *p2, 2/2 RC, p4; repeat from * to end.

Row 34: Repeat Row 4.

Row 35: Repeat Row 17.

Row 36: Repeat Row 2.

Repeat Rows 1 to 36.

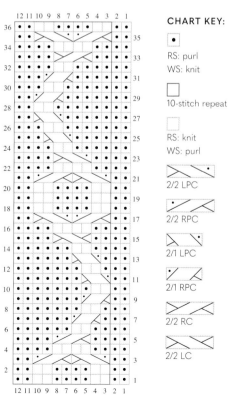

CHART KEY:

• RS: purl
WS: knit

□ 10-stitch repeat

□ RS: knit
WS: purl

2/2 LPC

2/2 RPC

2/1 LPC

2/1 RPC

2/2 RC

2/2 LC

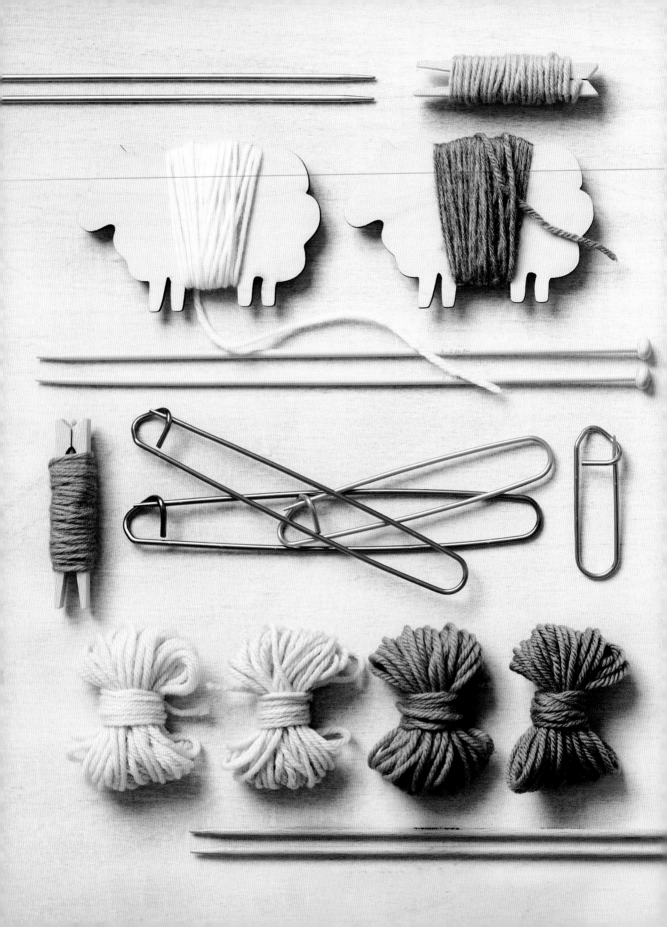

CHAPTER SEVEN

Cables: Essentials and Design

New to cables or need a refresher? In this chapter you'll learn all the key skills and techniques you need to start your twisting, winding journey, including tips on recognizing and avoiding errors, how to read and understand charts, and how to make sure your cables look how they should. When you're ready, you can explore how to use cables in your designs by learning about placement, choice of yarn, and why gauge is so important. Or take it to the next level by designing your own cables, taking inspiration from the world around you.

How to work cables

Cables are normally worked in stockinette (knit on RS rows, purl on the WS). This sets the smooth front of the stitch to face you on the RS of the work, giving a clear, well-defined edge to the cable.

To provide contrast and make the cable "pop," a different texture is needed for the background. Reverse stockinette (purl on RS rows, knit on the WS) is frequently used for this purpose because the bumpier appearance of the reverse stockinette provides strong contrast to the smoother stockinette fabric.

Of course, there are many variations and designers may incorporate rib stitches (alternating knits and purls), seed (moss) stitches (offset knits and purls), garter stitch (every row knit), lace, bobbles, and more. Cables can be simple or complex and may be combined together or used alone. Cables are frequently designed to be viewed from the RS but it is also possible to produce reversible cables.

Whatever type of cable you are working with, most cables follow a similar approach. This will involve taking one or more stitches and swapping the order of the stitch/stitches and working them in a different order. In its simplest form, this is achieved by transferring the stitches onto a small needle (a cable needle) and holding them in front of, or behind, the work. Stitches are then worked from the main needle before working the stitches that were held on the cable needle. With complex cables two cable needles may be required.

Some of the key cables are illustrated in this chapter. Wider or narrower cables are worked in the same way. Any unusual stitches or cables will be described in the key or in a separate stitch glossary (usually at the back of the book or end of the pattern).

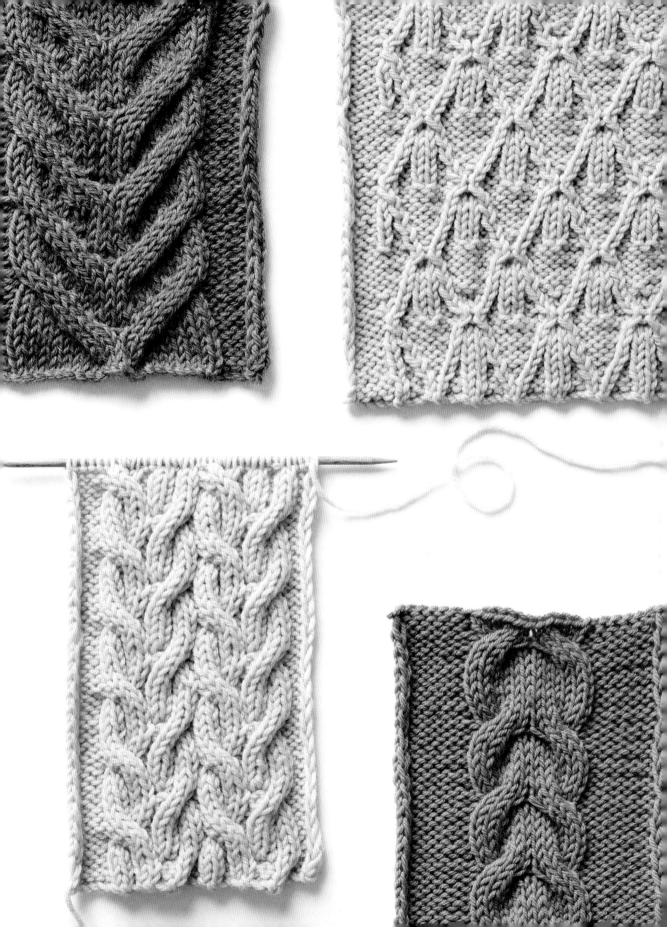

Tools and materials

Here you will find details of the equipment that will form the basis of your knitting workbag and a selection of other equipment that isn't essential but could be useful.

YARN

There are two main categories of yarn fiber—natural and synthetic. Natural fibers are divided into two categories: animal and vegetable. Animal fibers include wool, angora, cashmere, and silk; vegetable fibers include cotton, linen, and ramie. The stitch samples and projects in this book have been made using Cascade Yarns® 220 Superwash®, which is made from 100 percent wool to show the stitch patterns off to their best advantage and to enhance the texture and durability of the projects.

PAIRS OF KNITTING NEEDLES

Widely available and commonly used, single-pointed needles are sold in pairs and have a point at one end and a knurl, knob, or other stopper at the opposite end to prevent the stitches sliding off. Use these needles for knitting flat fabrics. When it comes to choosing your first needles, try as many different types, lengths, shapes, and materials as you can. The ball band that comes with your yarn is a good reference to check as it tells you the recommended knitting needle sizes and, in some cases, the recommended knitted gauge (see page 146).

STITCH HOLDERS

These long pins are used for holding groups of stitches until they are required—such as the top of a pocket opening.

STITCH MARKERS

These small plastic markers are used to mark a particular place along a row.

PEN, PENCIL, AND GRAPH PAPER

These essential items are useful for marking off where you are in a pattern, making notes about patterns, or assisting when designing patterns.

SCISSORS

Choose small scissors with sharp points because these will allow you to cut neatly and in the right place. It is worth investing in good-quality scissors, since inexpensive ones may snag your knitted fabric.

SEWING OR TAPESTRY NEEEDLES

Needles with sharper points, such as the type used for needlepoint or tapestry, are useful for sewing in ends where you need to split the yarn.

PINS

Pins are used to hold your knitting together when assembling. Choose large-headed pins where possible so that you can see them easily. A selection of longer pins for longer seams and shorter pins for smaller areas will be useful. Special T-pins are available for blocking knits. These have a T-shaped head, making them easier and safer to use vertically (as opposed to flat to the knitting).

Cable tools

Fortunately, cable knitting requires only a simple cable needle in addition to the usual knitting tools in your workbag. A cable needle is a short needle with points at both ends as a means of temporarily holding a small number of stitches. This allows the stitches to be transferred between the needles in either direction. If you don't have a cable needle to hand, a double-pointed needle (dpn) will be a good substitute. There are different types of cable needle so try a couple if you can and see which you prefer. Popular types are:

Straight a short needle with points at both ends. Frequently metal but may be plastic or wood.

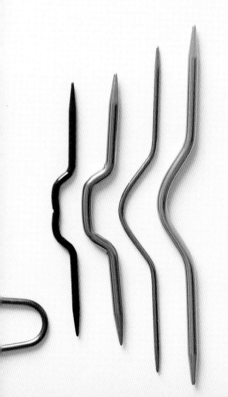

Cranked or kinked similar to the straight needle but with a small dip in the center that helps to hold the stitches in place. Available in metal, plastic, or wood.

Hook or "u" this type is less common but a good choice if you are working with a slippy yarn or complex cables as the hook hangs down, preventing the stitches from sliding off. These are usually plastic.

NOTE

Cable needles, like all knitting needles, come in different sizes. Choose one that is a similar size to the needles in your pattern or slightly smaller.

How patterns are presented

In most respects, cable designs follow the same format as any knitting pattern. Where there are cables in a pattern, these may be described in either chart or written form. In some patterns, there may be several charts that are used at different times and in different combinations. In this book, every pattern is illustrated in both chart and written formats.

Starting a cable pattern—set-up rows

Cables do create a certain amount of distortion in the fabric. This will frequently be the case at the cast-on or bound- (cast-) off edges but may occur elsewhere, such as the tops of sleeves.

To avoid possible distortion, a series of plain or simplified rows is frequently worked before any twists or crossed stitches are completed. This means that the pattern repeat may not begin on Row 1. Instead, a separate series of rows is worked just once before

the pattern repeat begins. These rows are the set-up rows. They allow for a little "breathing space" before the main pattern is introduced.

In a written pattern, set-up rows may be separately identified. However, in some patterns, the instructions will give you the set-up rows, then, once these rows and the first pattern repeat have been completed, the pattern will ask you to work from, for example, Row 5. In the example below, the pattern has four set-up rows and a 14-row pattern repeat. You are asked

to work Rows 1 to 18, then repeat Rows 5 to 12. The 14 rows (5 to 18) are the pattern repeat. Rows 1 to 4 are the set-up rows.

In a charted pattern, the set-up rows will normally be identified by a boxed outline in a different color to the main pattern repeat (see below in blue). The key will explain this. As with the written instructions, Rows 1 to 4 are worked just once, Rows 5 to 18 are repeated.

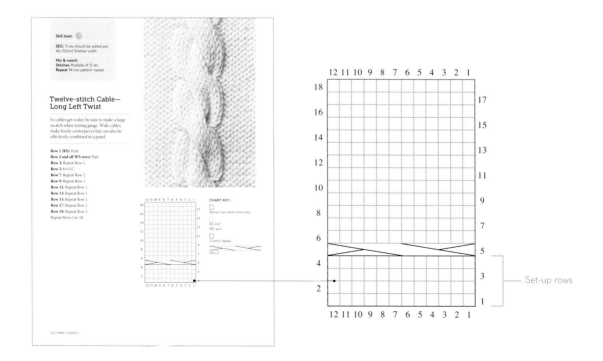

Pattern repeat

In order to create a cohesive design, a pattern will usually be made up of a series of rows that are repeated in sequence. This can be any number of rows depending on the complexity of the design. The sequence is referred to as the "pattern repeat." The written and chart instructions will show the pattern repeat.

On a chart, the pattern repeat will be indicated by an outline. In written instructions this will be indicated by the use of brackets or asterisks. The sections between the brackets or asterisks are worked one or more times until the end of a row or round.

In the chart illustration below, the pattern repeat is made up of 8 stitches and 11 rows. This is indicated in the chart by the red outline.

In the written instructions, the pattern asks you to repeat the section from the asterisk *. In some cases the pattern may state to repeat the section to the end of a row. This would be described as "repeat from * to end." It may also say to work a set number of times. For example, "repeat from * xxx times."

In some instances, there may be "edge stitches" which are outside the red outline (this is described in more detail on the next page). For these patterns you will see "repeat from * until xxx sts remain." At this point there will be a different instruction for the last few stitches (and sometimes the first few stitches) of the row. The pattern repeat is just the part between the asterisks.

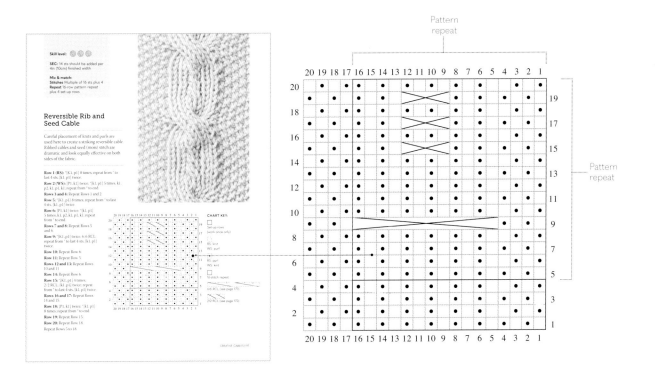

Edge stitches

In a charted design, the edge stitches are the ones that sit outside the red boxed outline. The stitches within the outline are worked multiple times but those outside the line are only worked once. There may be edges stitches at the beginning of the row, the end of the row, or at both ends of the row. There may not be edge stitches on every row and the number of stitches may vary according to the pattern.

When working cables, it isn't always practical, or possible, to work complete repeats of a pattern on every row. In this case, the pattern may feature edge stitches.

Edge stitches are partial repeats or even different stitches altogether that are worked just once at the beginning or end of a row. Edge stitches may be needed to allow for different sizes in garments; they are also used for neat shaping where a cable would otherwise sit too close to a decrease or increase and would make the fabric bulky or fussy.

Using edge stitches is also important in balancing complex all-over designs where cables intersect and there isn't an obvious place to pause the repeat.

In the chart below (on the left), the pattern has a simple repeat but needs to split the repeat at either edge to give it balance. The number of edge stitches is the same on each row.

In the written instructions the edge stitches are the ones outside the asterisked section.

INTERSECTING CABLES

Intersecting cables, on the other hand, don't easily lend themselves to a neat edge. In the pattern below the designer has added edge stitches. This creates a neat and tidy, balanced finish. Note how the repeat is not a simple boxed outline but varies on some rows. This is to allow for cables that travel over the course of a pattern repeat. You can see that with these designs the number of edge stitches varies as the cable travels to the edge of the panel.

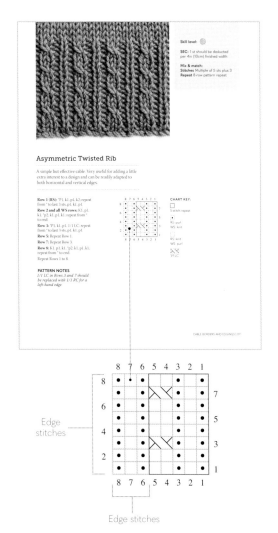

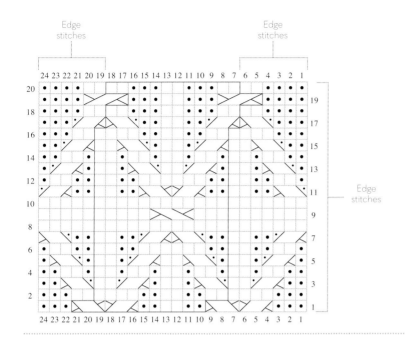

In the written version of the chart, the number of edge stitches varies in the same way. This is perhaps less obvious but it is the stitches worked outside the asterisked section that are only worked once (illustrated below in bold, for reference). Again, this may be at the start of the row, the end, both (or neither!).

Row 1 (RS): **P3, 2/1 RC, 2/1 LC,** *p2, k2, p2, 2/1 RC, 2/1 LC; repeat from * to last 3 sts, **p3.**

Rest rows

The term "rest rows" isn't usually used in patterns as such, but you may hear knitters refer to it. It simply means rows where no cables or twists are taking place. Often this will be the WS row but it can be a RS row if there are no cable or other pattern stitches being used.

You may also hear knitters use the term "knit the knits and purl the purls."

This can be a little confusing when knitting flat as it involves making a purl stitch where the previous row was knitted and vice versa. What it describes is the look of the stitch. Essentially, if there is a bump facing you, this stitch will be purled. If the stitch is smooth and the bump is on the side away from you, the stitch is knitted.

RS: Knit

WS: Purl

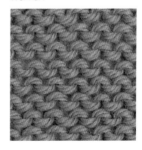

Cable rest row

RS

WS

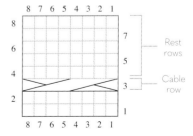

Understanding and following charts

Charts are a way of depicting pattern information in a graphical form. Charts are mainly used to depict the more complex parts of a design, and this is often the case with cables. Many knitters and designers find them helpful as they are more visually representative of the design and it is possible to see the pattern structure at a glance.

Symbols

Charts use symbols to represent different stitches. For a full list of symbols see pages 171–174.

Key

Each chart will be accompanied by a key. Always read the key before you begin as there is no standard set of symbols, and designers and publishers follow different conventions when producing charted patterns.

Take particular care to note any symbols that have a double use. For example, a blank white square will often be used to depict a knit stitch on a RS row and a purl stitch on a WS row. In other words, this would produce a stockinette fabric.

Purl stitches worked on a RS row may then have a separate symbol (often a solid black circle). On the WS, the same circle symbol is used to indicate that a knit stitch is worked when you

see this symbol on the chart. This will create a reverse stockinette fabric viewed from the RS.

As long as you follow the key, you should be fine, so don't worry if you see what are apparently two instructions for a single stitch type.

A key might look something like this (see full list of chart keys and abbreviations on pages 171–174):

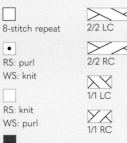

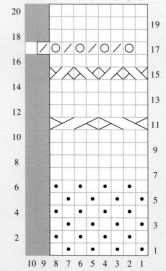

Squares and spans

Each square of a chart represents one stitch of knitting. Combinations of stitches, for example, cables or decreases, may span over a number of squares. This denotes that these stitches are worked as a unit.

No stitch

To make charts easier to produce, where a stitch is decreased (and so does not exist for the remainder of the section) a gray or black square is often used to depict "no stitch." In the example on the right, the equivalent written pattern would read as follows:

Row 1 (RS): *P1, k1; repeat from * to end.
Row 2 (WS): *K1, p1; repeat from * to end.
Rows 3 to 6: Repeat Rows 1 and 2.

Row 7: Knit.
Row 8: Purl.
Rows 9 and 10: Repeat Rows 7 and 8.
Row 11: *2/2 LC, 2/2 RC; repeat from * to end.
Row 12: Purl.
Row 13: Knit.
Row 14: Purl.
Row 15: *1/1 LC, 1/1 RC; repeat from * to end.
Row 16: Purl.
Row 17: K1, *yo, k2tog; repeat from * to last st, k1.
Row 18: Purl.
Row 19: Knit.
Row 20: Purl.
Repeat Rows 1 to 20.

In other words, the chart is read straight across, ignoring the gray squares.

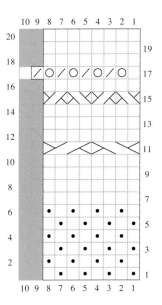

Row numbering

To save printing space and to make patterns easier to visualize, designs where alternate rows are all identical may not be shown on the chart. This will be clear from the row numbering (usually printed vertically up the side of the chart), where only every other row will be numbered. Alternatively, the key may have instructions to treat every alternate row as, for example, a purl row.

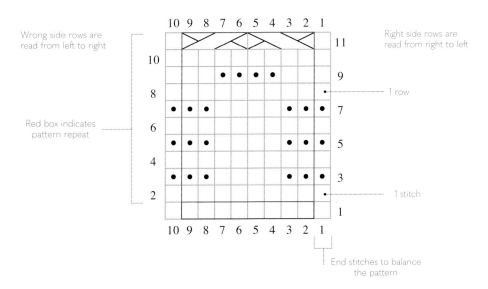

Wrong side rows are read from left to right

Right side rows are read from right to left

Red box indicates pattern repeat

1 row

1 stitch

End stitches to balance the pattern

Sizing

In garment patterns, a chart may have additional boxed-out or demarcated sections to depict the different instructions for different sizes.

Be careful to follow the correct section for your size. Here, if you were making the small size (knitted flat as a separate piece) you would work the first three rows as follows:

Row 1 (RS): *P1, k1, p1, k2; repeat from * to end.
Row 2: *P2, k1, p1, k1; repeat from * to end.
Row 3: As Row 1.

The medium size would read:
Row 1 (RS): *P1, k1, p1, k2; repeat from * to last 3 sts, p1, k1, p1.
Row 2: K1, p1, k1, *p2, k1, p1, k1; repeat from * to end.
Row 3: As Row 1.

And the large size would read:
Row 1 (RS): *P1, k1, p1, k2; repeat from * to last st, p1.
Row 2: K1, *p2, k1, p1, k1; repeat from * to end.
Row 3: As Row 1.

Multiple charts

It is rare for a chart to show an entire garment due to the size of chart this would require. Hence, where there are several areas of pattern in a piece, there will be several small charts. You will be instructed which chart to follow at the appropriate part in the text.

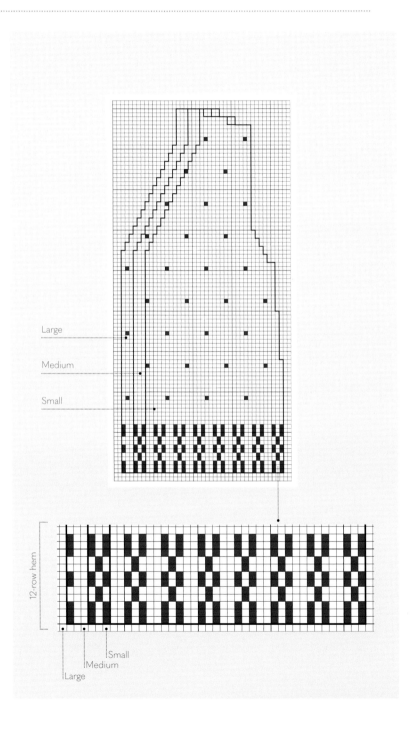

Knitting direction

Charts are used for both flat knitting and knitting in the round. The key difference in following these charts is in the direction of knitting and the order in which to read the chart.

FLAT KNITTING

Rows are normally worked starting at the bottom right corner and reading from right to left for the first row. The next row is then read starting at the left and reading from left to right.

CIRCULAR KNITTING

With projects knitted in the round, all rows (rounds) are read in the same direction, usually starting at the bottom right corner and reading from right to left.

This may seem confusing but if you visualize your knitting as you hold it, a flat piece is knitted from the right-hand edge to the left, swapped back into the left hand and knitted from left edge to right. By contrast, with a circular knit you are always knitting in the same direction, usually from right to left, and the work never swaps hands.

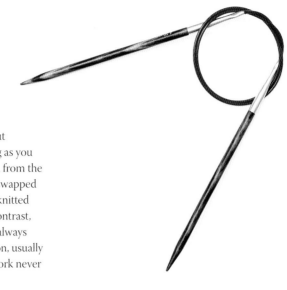

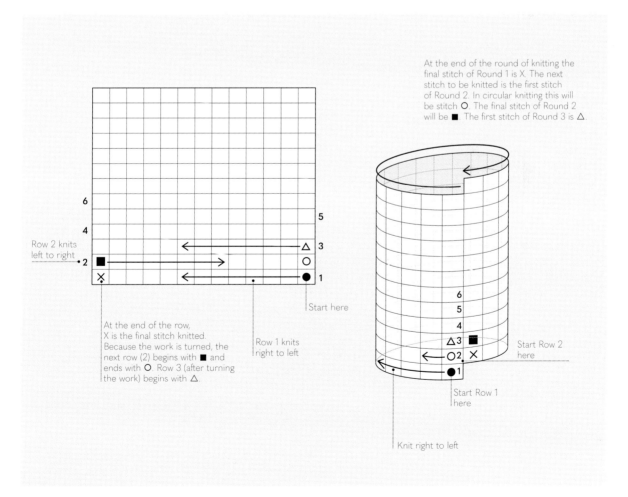

At the end of the round of knitting the final stitch of Round 1 is X. The next stitch to be knitted is the first stitch of Round 2. In circular knitting this will be stitch O. The final stitch of Round 2 will be ■. The first stitch of Round 3 is △.

Row 2 knits left to right

At the end of the row, X is the final stitch knitted. Because the work is turned, the next row (2) begins with ■ and ends with O. Row 3 (after turning the work) begins with △.

Row 1 knits right to left

Start here

Start Row 2 here

Start Row 1 here

Knit right to left

Gauge

A knitter's best friend, but also, arguably, the part of a project that knitters like the least, is gauge (tension). Mention gauge swatches (or gauge squares) to most knitters and wait for the groans! But, while they may seem like an annoyance that only serves to keep you away from your precious knitting project, they can save a lot of disappointment.

Gauge (tension) is simply the size (length × width) of a knitting stitch knitted on a specific size of needle using a specified technique. Because stitches form the basis of a knitted fabric, it stands to reason that if your stitches are larger or smaller than the ones knitted by the designer (usually if you knit more loosely or tighter), you may not produce a piece of knitting the same size as the one the designer knitted. If you doubt that this is the case, ask three of your knitting friends to each make a square using the same needles, rows, and stitches and compare the finished sizes. They will almost certainly be different. But does this matter? Small differences over a small square may not seem significant, but if your stitches are just an eighth bigger than the designer's, for every 100 stitches the designer casts on, your work will measure the equivalent of 12 stitches larger. On a shawl with 400 stitches, that's the equivalent of an extra 50 stitches without your having cast on a single extra stitch. Equally, if your square is smaller than the designer's, your garment will be correspondingly smaller—and the greater the difference, the smaller the garment will be.

So, on balance, as much as a gauge swatch seems like an obstacle designed to prevent you from getting stuck into your project, knitting one is a worthwhile exercise.

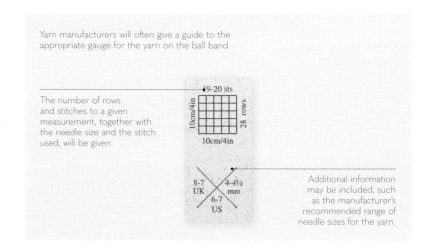

Yarn manufacturers will often give a guide to the appropriate gauge for the yarn on the ball band.

The number of rows and stitches to a given measurement, together with the needle size and the stitch used, will be given.

19-20 sts

10cm/4in

28 rows

10cm/4in

8-7 UK   4-4½ mm   6-7 US

Additional information may be included, such as the manufacturer's recommended range of needle sizes for the yarn.

Non-matching gauge

There are occasions when it is not possible to match both the number of rows and the number of stitches simultaneously. With one set of needles your rows are correct but you have too few stitches. However, when you go up a needle size, the stitch numbers are correct, but there are too few rows.

Because we all knit differently, it is quite common to find that you can't exactly match the gauge stated in a given pattern. If, having tried a couple of needle sizes, you find that you can't match both stitches and rows, it is generally advisable to ensure that the number of stitches is correct, even if this means that the number of rows is different from the pattern. Where the number of rows is different from the stated gauge, you may need to work

either fewer or more rows to achieve the correct dimensions. If the pattern gives measurements—for example, "knit until the work measures Xin/cm"—the number of rows isn't usually important, although you may not end in the same place on the pattern repeat. Where the pattern requires a specific number of rows, calculate what the length will be based on the stated gauge. Compare this to the length if you used your own gauge and aim to work more/fewer rows to match the original length. If it is a close measurement over a small length this may not be necessary, but over a long length, adjustments will be needed. Aim to adjust length in areas where there is no shaping, if at all possible. If adjusting rows in an area where stitches will be picked up, you may need to adjust the number of stitches being picked up accordingly.

Measuring gauge

Knit a swatch exactly according to the pattern, bearing in mind that you may be asked to work in a pattern stitch or in a simple stockinette stitch. Knit the swatch 10 or so stitches larger and work 10 rows more than the stated gauge. This allows you to measure in the center of the swatch, which is more accurate since edge stitches are rarely the same size as the main body of the fabric and can distort your calculations.

1. Bind (cast) off, wash, and block your swatch. Ideally, leave it overnight to allow the stitches to settle. Measuring in the center of the swatch, mark a line vertically, straight up one column of stitches, with a large-headed pin. Use a ruler to measure the stated width, usually 4in (10cm). Mark this measurement with a second pin. Count the stitches between the two pins. Include any half, quarter, or partial stitches.

2. Starting several rows into the swatch and in the center of the width, place a pin horizontally, straight along a row of stitches. Measure the stated length in a straight vertical line and mark this point with a second pin. Count the rows between the two pins including any partial rows. If your finished measurements match the pattern, you can start knitting with the needles you have been using. If the square is too small, repeat the process using needles a size larger. If the square is too large, try again with smaller needles.

Once you are ready to start your project, use the same needles as you did for your correct swatch and remember to adjust any smaller or larger needles for ribs or bands correspondingly.

TIPS

• If you are working with textured yarns it can be difficult to measure stitches and rows accurately. To remedy this, use a piece of smooth, contrasting thread and add it during knitting by inserting a lifeline (see page 160) after four or five rows. Lay a second piece of thread between the fourth and fifth stitches to mark out the edge and again after the number of stitches stated to be the correct gauge in the pattern. Run these threads up the sides of the work like a running stitch by taking them to the back after two rows and bringing them forward after a further two rows, and so on. Once the stated number of rows has been knitted, add a further lifeline. Use these lines to measure your work.

• Label swatches and keep them for future reference in a folder or box. They may come in handy if you knit the project or use the same yarn again.

• Swatches can be made into projects such as coasters, mats, or small purses. They can also be sewn together to create a blanket—a fun history of your knitting projects!

• If a pattern is to be knitted in the round, make sure you knit your gauge swatch in the round, since gauge is often different when comparing circular to flat knitting.

Cable examples

Cables follow similar principles and once you have mastered the essential movements it should be straightforward to follow the instructions provided in the glossary on pages 171–174 (or alongside the stitch pattern). These are some examples of standard cable techniques as well as a couple of more unusual stitches that you may want to incorporate in your designs.

Four-stitch cable left on a background of reverse stockinette (2/2 LC) ⬗⬗

For this cable the stitches are held to the front of the work and the movement is from right to left. It may also be described as "cable left," "cable cross left," or "cable twist left."

1

1. Purl to start of cable. Hold cable needle in RH, slightly above and parallel to RH needle and slip next 2 stitches onto cable needle as if to purl (purlwise).

2. Hold cable needle with stitches on at front of work. With a hooked cable needle simply allow needle to drop to front of work. For straight or cranked cable needles, support cable needle in RH or very carefully poke needle into fabric, taking care not to split yarn or snag fabric.

3. With working yarn at back, knit next 2 stitches from LH needle as normal. Avoid a hole at crossover point by drawing up yarn quite firmly after first stitch. These stitches may feel tight and quite difficult to work. Don't worry, this is normal!

4

4. Leave LH needle at back of work. With cable needle in LH, knit 2 stitches from cable needle. Be careful to keep stitches in same order and don't twist stitches when lifting cable needle.

5

5. When 2 stitches from cable needle have been worked, this completes the left front cable. Purl to end of row.

Four-stitch cable right on a background of reverse stockinette (2/2 RC) ⊠ ⊠

To create a cable that moves from left to right, the cable stitches are held to the back of the work. This technique may also be described as "cable right," "cable cross right," or "cable twist right."

1. Purl to start of cable. Hold cable needle in RH, slightly above and parallel to RH needle and slip next 2 stitches onto cable needle as if to purl (purlwise).

2. Hold cable needle with stitches on at back of work. With a hooked cable needle simply allow needle to drop to back of work. For straight or cranked cable needles, support cable needle in RH or very carefully poke needle into fabric, taking care not to split yarn or snag fabric.

3. With working yarn at back, knit next 2 stitches from LH needle as normal. Avoid a hole at crossover point by drawing up yarn quite firmly after first stitch. These stitches may feel tight and quite difficult to work. Don't worry, this is normal!

4. Leave LH needle at back of work. With cable needle in LH, knit 2 stitches from cable needle. Be careful to keep stitches in same order and don't twist stitches when lifting cable needle.

5. When 2 stitches from cable needle have been worked, this completes the right back cable. Purl to end of row.

2

Twelve-stitch ribbed cable left on a background of reverse stockinette (6/6 LC)

This wider cable incorporates ribbing for the cable. The beauty of ribbed cables is that they are reversible, making them ideal for projects where both sides of the fabric may be visible.

1. Work to start of cable. Hold cable needle in RH, slightly above and parallel to RH needle, and slip next 6 stitches onto cable needle as if to purl (purlwise).

2. Hold cable needle with stitches on to front of work.

3. With working yarn at back, work the next stitches from LH needle in rib (k1, p1) 3 times.

4. Leave LH needle at back of work. With cable needle in LH work stitches from cable needle in rib (k1, p1) 3 times.

RS (reverse stockinette background)

WS (stockinette background)

4

5. When 6 stitches from cable needle have been worked, this completes the cable. Work to end of row.

6. The rows that form the cable will be worked throughout in rib to produce a reversible cable. Note, however, that the background is not truly reversible.

Twelve-stitch ribbed cable right on a background of seed (moss) stitch (6/6 RC) ⊏▭▱▱▭▭⊐

For a fully reversible fabric, ribbed cables can be paired with a reversible stitch for the background. Here, seed (moss) stitch has been used instead of the reverse stockinette. Double seed stitch or garter stitch would also make good choices.

1. Work to start of cable. Hold cable needle in RH, slightly above and parallel to RH needle, and slip next 6 stitches onto cable needle as if to purl (purlwise).

2. Hold cable needle with stitches on at back of work.

3. With working yarn at back, work the next stitches from LH needle in rib (k1, p1) 3 times.

4. Leave LH needle at back of work. With cable needle in LH work stitches from cable needle in rib (k1, p1) 3 times.

5. When 6 stitches from cable needle have been worked, this completes the cable. Work to end of row.

6. The rows that form the cable will be worked throughout in rib to produce a reversible cable. Here, as the ribbed cable is set on a seed (moss) stitch background it will produce a fully reversible fabric.

2

Nine-stitch left cable worked with two cable needles (4/1/4 LC) ⟥⟨⟩⟨⟩⟤

Where two cables cross with a third set of stitches intersecting these are referred to as "axis" cables. For these cables it may be necessary to separate the stitches on the cable needle and move the cable needle from back to front (or vice versa) before completing the stitch. This example of a nine-stitch left cable shows one way to do this.

1. Work to start of cable. Slip next 4 stitches onto cable needle as if to purl (purlwise).
2. Hold cable needle with stitches on at front of work.
3. Slip next stitch from LH needle onto a second cable needle.

4. Hold second cable needle at back of work.
5. Knit next 4 stitches from LH needle.

6. Knit next stitch from back cable needle.

7. Knit 4 stitches from front cable needle.
8. Once a few rows have been worked, you can see how this cable looks in practice.

Nine-stitch right cable worked with one cable needle (4/1/4 RC) ⊏▭▭✕▭▭⊐

With some axis cables, where two cables cross with a third set of stitches intersecting, two cable needles may be used. This example of a nine-stitch right cable shows one way to do this.

1. Work to start of cable. Slip next 5 stitches onto cable needle as if to purl (purlwise).
2. Hold cable needle with stitches on at back of work.

3. With working yarn at back, knit next 4 stitches from LH needle.

4. Slip 1 stitch from cable needle to LH needle.
5. Bring cable needle to front of work.

Pinch to hold stitches

6. Knit next stitch from LH needle.
7. Knit 4 stitches from cable needle.
8. Once a few rows have been worked, you can see how this cable looks in practice.

WORKING CABLES WITHOUT A CABLE NEEDLE

Cables can be made without using a cable needle at all. Instead, the stitches are moved by manipulating them with your fingers. As this technique can result in laddered stitches, it is worth practicing on your swatch so you know how careful you need to be with the yarn.

Infinity cable examples

Infinity cables are so-called as they have no beginning and end. They are used where the cable starts in the middle of a fabric and enable "floating" cables to be made. Infinity cables are slightly different from regular cables in that they require multiple increases and decreases in order to create smoother curves and loops and to avoid bumpy joins.

Five-stitch infinity cable— multiple increases

The bottom of the infinity circle is created with multiple increases. It is worked on the RS of the fabric.

STAGE ONE—MAKE ONE INCREASE

1. Work to start of cable. Use tip of LH needle and insert under strand between two needles from front to back.

2. Knit into back of strand.
3. Allow new stitch to drop off LH needle (1 stitch increased).

STAGE TWO—CENTRAL DOUBLE INCREASE

4. Insert RH needle into back of next stitch on LH needle.

5. Knit stitch but don't allow to drop off LH needle.

6. Bring RH needle to front and knit into front of same stitch.
7. Allow stitch to drop off LH needle (2 stitches increased).

8. Insert LH needle from back to front into loop below stitch just worked on RH needle.

9. Knit stitch and allow to drop off LH needle (3 stitches increased).

10. Repeat steps 1–3. Four stitches increased in total.

STAGE THREE—MULTIPLE DECREASES

At this point the multiple increases have been completed and there are two stitches forming the right strand of the cable, a central stitch that will be the "filling," and two stitches to form the left strand.

The next rows are worked as normal cables without increasing any further stitches until the circle is ready to be completed.

To complete the circle we need to return the stitches to the original number. We do this by making a series of multiple decreases on the WS of the fabric.

11. Work to start of cable. Slip next 3 stitches purlwise onto RH needle.
12. Use LH needle to lift second stitch on RH needle over first.
13. Drop lifted stitch off RH needle (1 stitch decreased).
14. Transfer first stitch on RH needle purlwise to LH needle.

15. Use RH needle to lift second stitch on LH needle over first.
16. Allow lifted stitch to drop off LH needle (2 stitches decreased).
17. Transfer first stitch on LH needle purlwise to RH needle.
18. Repeat steps 2–6 (4 stitches decreased).
19. Knit remaining slipped stitch on LH needle. Work to end of row as normal.
20. After a few rows of reverse stockinette have been worked, you'll see a circle with smooth curves at the bottom and top.

Part-completed circle ready for multiple decreases.

Seven-stitch infinity cable— multiple increases

For a wider cable it is necessary to increase additional stitches. For a cable with three stitches on each strand there will be three stitches on each strand plus a central stitch, making even stitches in total. Because there are a large number of increases, this is worked over two rows, the first our on the RS row, then a second set of two on the purl row.

3

STAGE ONE AND TWO—MULTIPLE INCREASES ON RS AND WS ROWS

1. RS row increases—work these as for the five-stitch infinity cable (see pages 154–155).
2. WS row increases.
3. Purl into next sttich as normal but don't allow stitch to drop off LH needle.

4. Wrap yarn counter-clockwise around RH needle.
5. Purl into same stitch.
6. Allow stitch to drop from LH needle (2 stitches increased).

Once the increases have been completed, the following row includes purling into the back loop of the yarn over. This is not an increase but it closes up the hole that the yarn over would otherwise leave. The work now continues with a pair of three-stitch strands and a central filling.

STAGE THREE—MULTIPLE DECREASES

When it is time to complete the circle, this will decrease the work from 7 stitches back down to 1 stitch.

4

7. Hold yarn at back and slip next 4 stitches purlwise to RH needle.

8. With LH needle lift second stitch on RH needle over first stitch.

9. Transfer first stitch from RH needle purlwise back to LH needle.

10. Use RH needle to lift second stitch on LH over first stitch.

11. Slip first stitch purlwise from LH needle back to RH needle.

12. Repeat steps 2–4 twice more.

13. Knit remaining slipped stitch. Work to end of row as normal.

14. After a few rows of reverse stockinette have been worked, you'll see a circle with smooth curves at the bottom and top.

Part-completed circle ready for multiple decreases.

Horizontal cable example

For more complex cables, particularly knots, it is useful to be able to work horizontal cable stitches. However, as cables are normally knitted vertically this requires a special approach.

ROW 1

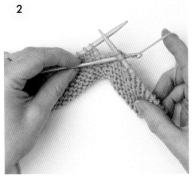

1. Work to where cable begins. Knit next 2 stitches.
2. Using crochet hook, insert hook from front to back into RH stitch and draw loop through to front.

3. Repeat for LH stitch.
4. Transfer 2 stitches onto LH needle, arranging stitches so that they are not twisted. Knit these 2 new stitches.

5. Slip same 2 stitches back to the LH needle.

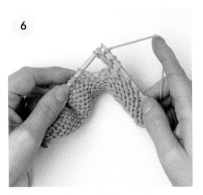

6. Yarn over (yarn will be coming from LH needle at first).

7. Knit next stitch, ssk.

8. Slip last 3 stitches just worked back to LH needle.
9. Knit into the back then the front of next stitch (again yarn will be coming from LH needle at first), k1, ssk.
10. Repeat steps 8–9 until cable is desired length but work final decrease as p2tog instead of ssk.

BIND (CAST) OFF ROW 1

1. Pass the stitches of horizontal cable back to LH needle, up to 2 beginning knit stitches, which are still on RH needle.

2. On the RH needle, pass the second stitch over the first.

3. Slip next stitch on LH to RH needle.
4. Repeat from Row 2 until you have also slipped a stitch over p2tog.
5. Work across rest of row. The horizontal cable takes up the row on which it was worked, and covers the row below it.

NOTE

The first stitches worked in the cable may initially look loose but should improve as the work progresses. Be sure not to pull the yarn tightly around the back of the work, or to work the cable tightly, as that will flatten it out. There will be an additional stitch.

ROW 2

1. Work to cable, then pick up and knit through back loop of each bound- (cast-) off stitch to replace it.

2. K2tog to return stitch count back to what it was before.

Tips, tricks, and errors

Even the most experienced knitters make mistakes. But fortunately there are some tips and tricks you can use to avoid making them, and if you know how to recognize a mistake, it is usually straightforward to correct it with a few simple techniques.

Using "lifelines"

Lifelines come in handy when you are learning a new pattern or technique because they allow you to pull the stitches off the needles and rip back to where you know the work was correct. A lifeline is a piece of smooth, contrasting-color yarn—a good 20in (50cm) or so longer than the knitting when fully stretched out—fine enough to go through the stitches without distorting them, but strong enough not to break.

To insert a lifeline, decide where you want your marking point to be—often, the first row of a pattern repeat. Thread your lifeline yarn onto a blunt yarn needle. Thread the yarn needle through the stitches on the knitting needle. Don't split the stitches as you go through, since this may damage the yarn and make it more difficult to unravel the work if needed.

Continue knitting your pattern. If you need to use your lifeline, take all the stitches off the needle and pull back the work to the lifeline row. Insert the tip of your knitting needle (or smaller needle, if necessary) into each stitch, following the lifeline exactly, however odd it may look. With the stitches back on the knitting needle, you can restart. Lifelines stay in the work until you are finished, or can be removed once you are happy that a section is correct, placing a new lifeline at the start of the next pattern repeat.

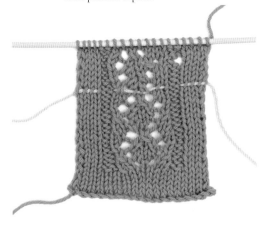

Counting rows

Counting cables presents a particular challenge as it is not easy to see which is the exact row where the twist has taken place. One way to deal with this is to use lifelines (see above). However, this can be time-consuming if the row repeat is short. A useful alternative is to use a padlock-style stitch marker and place it two or three stitches before you make the cable twist. If you lose count, you can go back to the marker and count the rows worked as for a normal stockinette or garter stitch fabric, confident that the marker is the start of the cable row (but easier to count!).

COUNTING STOCKINETTE AND REVERSE STOCKINETTE

Each V represents one row. Exclude the cast-on row and the row on the needles when counting. Reverse stockinette rows are counted in the same way, counting from the knit (smooth) face.

COUNTING GARTER STITCH

Each pairing of a peak with a trough represents two rows. As with stockinette stitch, ignore the cast-on and bound- (cast-) off rows on the needles when counting.

Spotting and avoiding errors

The sooner a mistake is spotted the less work is involved in putting it right. The most common errors arise from misinterpreting patterns and not reading ahead. Once you are knitting, dropped stitches, extra stitches, losing your place, and miscounting or misreading a pattern account for most knitting problems.

INTERPRETING PATTERNS

Frustrating though it may seem, there is no standard set of knitting pattern abbreviations or chart symbols. It is recommended to read all the pattern notes and abbreviations before starting, even if you are an experienced knitter. If you're not sure what the designer means by a particular term, don't guess! Check any books you may have or search the internet for explanations of techniques that aren't familiar. In some cases, there may be contact details for the designer or errata may be made available online.

READING AHEAD

Many errors can be avoided by reading patterns thoroughly and by reading ahead. Of course, it isn't necessary to memorize an entire pattern, but it is worth watching out for unusual instructions and in particular, sections where two or more actions are taking place at the same time.

CABLE AND TRAVELING STITCH PATTERNS

Common errors with cables occur when counting the number of straight rows between twist rows. Marking up rows on a photocopied or redrawn chart will help to avoid this kind of error. Making sure that twists move in the correct direction is another point to watch out for. Cable directions are normally determined by whether the cable stitches are held at the front or back of the work. The only real way to be sure is to review your knitting after each twist row, using the pattern picture as well as the pattern instructions as a guide.

TIPS

- Photocopy your pattern and note any areas with multiple or unusual instructions.
- If necessary, write out or chart any rows with multiple instructions.
- Work in good light, particularly if you're using dark yarn, or where the colors in a project are similar.
- Use a highlighter pen or soft pencil to mark off rows on your chart as you complete each one. Row counters or sticky notes (placed below the row you are working on) are also a good way of keeping track. Avoid crossing out rows using permanent markers, in case you need to read it again later.

COLORWORK AND STITCH PATTERNS

Colorwork and stitch patterns are best checked on a regular basis by comparing the work to the illustration and pattern/chart.

USING STITCH MARKERS

Stitch markers should be used to make sure that you have the correct number of stitches before and after any pattern repeats. They should also be used to check that each pattern repeat has been correctly completed. Place a marker at the start of the first repeat, at the start of each subsequent repeat, and at the end of the final repeat. Used correctly, stitch markers should limit any stitch-count errors to one row. However, bear in mind that this doesn't necessarily eliminate any pattern errors within the repeat. It is also worth checking that there will be the same number of stitches in each repeat throughout.

FIXING A PATTERN STITCH ERROR

Cable stitches can be dropped as a unit. Place a safety pin or stitch holder through the left leg of each stitch in the row below the incorrect row. Drop and unravel all the affected stitches down to the holder. Correct the stitches as required using the stitches on the holder as the base row (this may involve using a cable needle to twist the stitches if cable stitches are involved); then use a crochet hook to lift the stitches individually back onto the needles.

Designing your own cables

To accompany the stitches in this book, you can also create your own cables and turn them into stunning designs.

Finding inspiration

Cables are often worked as panels or motifs and many are inspired by Celtic and Irish knots or traditional symbols from folklore. Runes are a great source of ideas for cables, and there are many beautifully illustrated books, such as the *Book of Kells*, that will give you endless ideas. Knotwork also has a strong tradition around the globe—you will find intricate patterns in Chinese art, stained glass, African textiles, and more.

You can look for ideas in books or designs by calligraphers who specialize in creating symbols for illuminated manuscripts and calligraphy work.

There is also plenty of inspiration to be found in the natural and built environment. Trees and bark, plants and leaves, waves and rivers, and even animals, can deliver some brilliant ideas. For the built environment, gates, fences, arches, brickwork, ironwork, and even manhole covers can be a fascinating source of shapes and patterns.

Going from idea to design

Once you have identified an image or idea, sketch it out on paper or in a computer drawing program. If you're not confident about drawing, you could also take a photograph and print it out, then use tracing paper to outline the key features for your design. If you're handy with computer software, you could import your image and digitally trace over it.

Step 1: Identify your image.

Step 2: Sketch it out on paper or trace over a print out or photo.

Step 3: Follow the steps in the next few pages until you have finished your cable!

The ins, outs, unders, and overs of cables

An important part of cable structure is the placement of the strands and whether a strand goes over or under its neighbor. The way in which these overs and unders are combined will dramatically change the look of the finished cable.

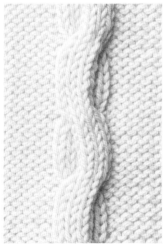

Compare these two cable examples. On the far left, the twist is always to the left and the twists are worked close together. This creates a rope-type effect—a very classic cable.

When the same two strands are twisted such that one strand or "leg" twists left then right, one cable will sit on top of the other. This can be seen in the cable on the left.

Visualizing the finished cable

A great way to visualize cables is to use string or i-cord and a cork or foam board with knitters' graph paper underneath, and pin out the shapes. This will allow you to see how the strands look in three dimensions, showing the unders and overs, and giving the closest replication of how the finished cable will look.

TIP

Using a different color yarn or string for each strand makes it quite straightforward to visualize the interplay between the cable strands and convert the cable into a charted form.

If you have a machine (mechanical or manual) for making i-cord, you can make several strands of i-cord in different colors.

Sketching your design

To ensure your design looks the correct shape when knitted, the quickest way is to sketch it out using knitters' graph paper. There are various sites online where you can print free, customized graph paper. Knitting software programs may also offer this option. It is possible to use ordinary square graph paper, however, as knit stitches are rectangular rather than square, drawing the shapes directly onto square graph paper may result in distorted cables.

1. Pin out your design using i-cord/string.

2. Leaving your i-cord in place, draw around it so that you have a design on the graph paper that is in the correct ratio.

3. Check that you have completed the outline then carefully unpin each section where the i-cord crosses and make a pencil line to show wherever the cord goes on top.

4. Repeat for each crossover, marking just the strands that go over the top of another strand.

5. This will give you the key points for your cable. You can now remove the i-cord.

6. Use a soft pencil to mark out the cables and where you plan to make the crossovers.

7. Once you have created your chart (see opposite), knit your swatch according to your chart. Be prepared to be flexible as it may be necessary to tweak or simplify your design.

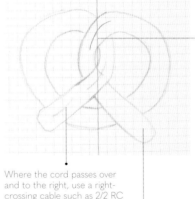

Where the cord passes over and to the right, use a right-crossing cable such as 2/2 RC or 2/1 RC; this moves the cord over to the right.

Where the cord passes over and to the left, use a left-crossing cable such as 2/2 LC or 2/1 LC; this moves the cord over to the left.

Axis cables (see page 152) are used where we want cables to crossover while keeping the central stitch. For example, a 2/1/2 RC is an axis cable, where the middle "1" splits the two cables on either side.

TIP

If you're designing a large motif, print out several sheets and join them together with tape.

Swatching for success

To work out the correct ratio for your graph paper, begin with a gauge (tension) swatch.

1. Work out your gauge using the yarn and needles you intend to use for your design. Knit a stockinette stitch swatch with this yarn and needles. Your swatch should be at least 4in (10cm) square.

2. Print out the graph paper according to the gauge (see page 146 for information on calculating gauge) so the number of boxes equate to the number of stitches and rows.

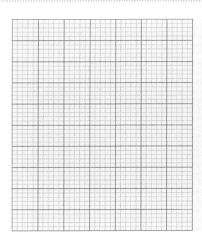

TIP

As the proportions will vary depending on the stitch pattern, yarn used, and gauge, we have illustrated our stitches using squares (ordinary graph paper) throughout this book. However, we would recommend creating correctly proportioned charts for each project to avoid distortions in the finished design. The pretzel is shown below using ordinary graph paper and knitters' graph paper, which is recommend when designing.

Creating a chart using knitters' graph paper

Once you have sketched out your cable you will need to convert it into chart form. Translating your drawing into a pattern requires an understanding of which stitches to use to create the desired effects. Here, the pretzel shape has been created using increase techniques such as the m1, inc1to5, m1, where a rapid increase is required to create the open centers at each side of the pretzel. These increases also allow the cable to curve to both the left and right.

CHART USING SQUARE GRAPH PAPER

At the top of the curve, we need to decrease multiple stitches in one row to return the stitches to the original count and also to round off the top of the curve.

Right and left twisting cables are used at the top edge to form the upper curve of the pretzel.

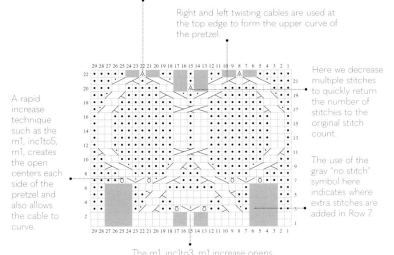

A rapid increase technique such as the m1, inc1to5, m1, creates the open centers each side of the pretzel and also allows the cable to curve.

Here we decrease multiple stitches to quickly return the number of stitches to the original stitch count.

The use of the gray "no stitch" symbol here indicates where extra stitches are added in Row 7.

The m1, inc1to3, m1 increase opens out the lower edge of the pretzel and makes stitches available for the central crossing cords.

CHART USING KNITTERS' GRAPH PAPER TO GET THE CORRECT PROPORTIONS

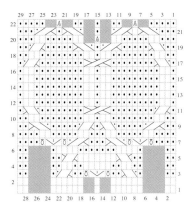

Combining cables

In addition to designing single cables, many patterns use several cables, putting them together to form a larger panel. Use the "mix and match" section (see opposite) to help you decide which cables will work readily together. There are many exciting options but we have included some suggestions below to get you started.

Simple pairing, mirroring, and alignment

A four-stitch cord may be paired with a honeycomb (1); two six-stitch cables may be placed together, working one as a left-twist and one as a right-twist to give an interesting, mirrored effect (2). A cable with a 12-row repeat can be placed alongside a cable with a 6-row repeat (3). This will result in two short cable repeats alongside a single, taller cable. Cables can also be offset or syncopated. These cables will not align, which can be interesting but more care is required when planning the start and end of the panel.

NOTE

To avoid very large charts, patterns may be broken down into smaller, more compact charts. The pattern will indicate which chart to work at each stage.

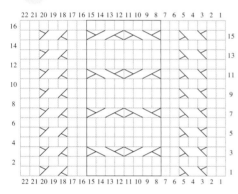

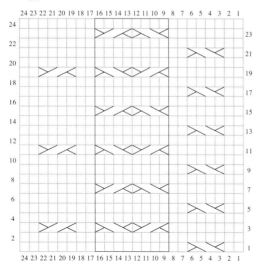

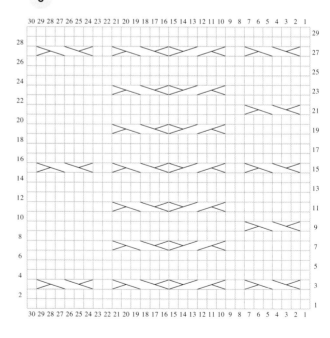

Mix and match

To make choosing your patterns easier, we have included a "mix and match" summary with each pattern that includes the stitch and row repeat. This means that you will be able to tell at a glance how many repeats you would need to align two or more cables. For example, a cable with a 2-row repeat will work well with almost any cable that is divisible by two. A 4-row repeat will work well with a cable that divides by four; 6-row cables will match readily with a cable that divides by six.

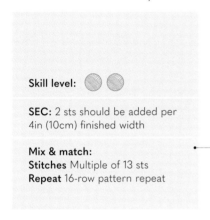

Skill level:

SEC: 2 sts should be added per 4in (10cm) finished width

Mix & match:
Stitches Multiple of 13 sts
Repeat 16-row pattern repeat

These panels can be found at the top of each pattern.

Example:
If you are using a 2-row cable alongside a 4-row cable, the two patterns will align every four rows, so rows 4, 8, 12, 16, and so on.

If you are using a 4-stitch cable alongside a 6-row cable, the two patterns will only align on rows that are divisible by both four and six—so rows 12, 24, 36, and so on.

A 6-stitch and an 8-stitch cable will align on rows 24, 48 (or wherever the row count is divisible by both six and eight).

Plotting your cables on graph paper will help you to judge where your cables will align and from there you can decide how to deal with any "leftover" rows if two cables don't match but you really want to pair them together!

Cable placement, drape, and shape

An equally important part of designing with cables is placement. This involves a combination of what is aesthetically pleasing but also how the cables affect the fabric. For example, a dense, heavily textured cable will create a stiffer fabric with less drape. This type of fabric would be ideal for a pillow or bag but would need careful swatching before including it in a garment.

Placing a dense cable in the center of a garment may cause it to pull in the fabric around it and affect the body and raise the hemline in the center. One way to avoid this would be to add a balancing cable at either side to raise up the edges to allow for the extra weight.

Cables can be used as a design feature when considering shaping. A block of simple, classic cables at the waistline of a long sweater dress can create a very attractive, gently curving silhouette without needing to disrupt the pattern with increases

and decreases; cabled edgings give stability when an edging is required that doesn't curl.

With garments it can be useful to cut out paper shapes of the main pieces and lay your swatch/es on the paper shapes. Knit each cable up as a separate swatch so you can really get creative and experiment with how your cables will look together. You can pin them together to give a rough idea of shape and drape. When making your paper pieces, don't forget to allow for seams and any ease (how close-fitting or loose the garment will be).

TOP

For your first design, a project with minimal or no shaping is a good idea. A pillow cover, afghan, wrap, or scarf would be good choices.

TIP

It isn't necessary to stick to conventional layouts. Try cables along hemlines and cuffs, in collars and necklines, or take cables from the hemline and extend them into the main body of the garment. You can also explore cable widths and spacing, or include a cable as a side panel insert rather than a center panel. There are so many possibilities!

Choosing the right yarn and needles

Once you have designed your cable, you will need to decide on a good yarn and the right size of needles to give it maximum impact.

Yarn texture

Cables are ideally suited to smooth but "grippy" yarns. Wool or wool-blend yarns are perfect as they give good stitch definition but also have a little grip. The natural plumpness of wool makes stitches appear more even and fills in any small gaps that may appear around cable edges. With cotton and similar yarns, the smooth texture of the yarn focuses the eye on the cable and makes it stand out. However, the lack of elasticity can make heavier cables droopy and holes may be more noticeable. Heathered and textured yarns can also look effective but the cables will be more subtle.

This eyelet cable has been knitted in sportweight (DK) yarn using US 5 (3.75mm) needles. The eyelet holes are clearly visible and the overall look is bulky.

The same eyelet cable worked in fine mohair using US 8 (5mm) needles is delicate and pretty, but the patterning is less visible.

Yarn color

Traditionally, cables are worked in off-white, which is an excellent choice. However, it isn't the only option, and you needn't feel limited to white/cream or even just pastels. Very dark colors and multicolored yarns can reduce the impact of cable patterns but there are many colors that will look great. The key is to swatch your pattern and see what works.

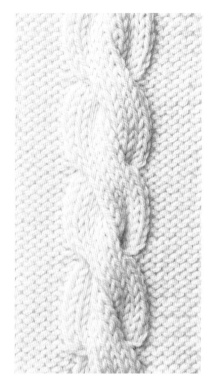

Needles

Commercial yarns normally specify a range of needle sizes and it's a good idea to use this as a starting point. Needles that are too large will create a fabric that will be looser and more open, which can reduce the impact of the design. Working on too small a needle may make knitting difficult and the combination of tighter stitches and the denser fabric of the cable may affect the handle and drape of the finished fabric.

Mohair yarn worked in stockinette stitch (30 stitches x 70 rows) has been knitted on the recommended needles (US 6/4mm), producing a neat and even fabric.

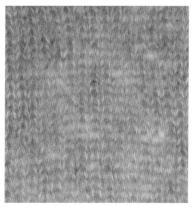

The same mohair yarn knitted on larger needles (US 10/6mm) creates a more open, looser stitch (20 stitches x 35 rows).

Stockinette and cables—the stockinette equivalent calculation (SEC)

Stockinette stitch and cables rarely share the same gauge (tension). The twisting and manipulation of the cables causes the fabric to be a little tighter and there are normally fewer stitches per inch in stockinette when compared to the same number of stitches worked in a cable pattern. This means that if a cable is introduced into an existing pattern, the fabric will be narrower. In some cases the difference won't be significant but it's always best to check!

To save you time, we have included the stockinette equivalent for each stitch pattern. This information tells you how many stitches you will need to add in order to substitute a cable into your pattern. We have calculated our numbers using a sample of 4in (10cm) as this is the standard size for a gauge swatch. Follow the formula (right) to calculate the SEC.

If your SEC is 9, this means that for every 4in (10cm) of width, you should add 9 stockinette stitches. The extra stitches could be at the edges of the pattern or within the cable or cable repeat.

Occasionally, the SEC will be a negative number. This is usually the case where a cable includes a wide stitch like garter or seed (moss) stitch. As these stitches spread rather than contract, you should deduct the stated number of SEC stitches for every 4in (10cm) of pattern.

Will the yarn type and needle size affect the SEC?

In most cases no. Providing you are swatching both your cable and your stockinette using the same yarn and needles as you need for your pattern, the stitches should be in the same ratio and so should require the same number of extra (or fewer) stitches per 4in (10cm).

How is the SEC calculated?

If you are using a cable from another book or a pattern of your own design and want to work out your own SEC, begin by swatching both fabrics. Swatch at least two repeats of the cable and a similar-sized swatch in stockinette. Then measure the two swatches and compare the rows and stitches per inch.

The SEC is calculated as follows:
1. Stockinette swatch width = number of stitches per 4in (10cm) = (A)
2. Cable swatch width = (B)
3. Number of stitches in cable (C)
4. $(A/B) \times (C)$ = number of cable stitches required to make a swatch the same size as the stockinette swatch (D)
5. The number of extra stitches required per 4in (10cm) to match the two is $D - A = E$

Worked example:
A: Stockinette swatch = 20 sts in 4in (10cm)
B: Cable width = 3in (7.6cm)
C: Number of stitches in cable = 28
D: $4/3 \times 28 = 37.3$ (round down to 37)
E: $37 - 20 = 17$
So we need to add 17 stitches for every 4in (10cm) width of knitting worked in our cable pattern to make it the same width as a piece of knitting worked in stockinette.

The same process can be done for rows, measuring the number of rows in each swatch, finding how many rows there are per inch, and working out the difference between the two.

If the calculation produces a negative number this means that there are more stockinette stitches than cable stitches per inch. In this case, we would need to deduct the number of stitches per inch to produce two swatches that are the same size.

Symbols, stitches, and abbreviations

To keep patterns compact, in both written and charted instructions, each stitch is given a symbol and an abbreviation.

Some pattern abbreviations are simple and obvious (k for knit, p for purl, for example). For cables, more detailed abbreviations may be used which can look confusing. However, they do normally follow the structure of the stitch. For example, a C4R represents a cable 4 that extends over four stitches in total and produces a cable that twists to the right. This may also be abbreviated to C4B (cable 4 back) which means that the cable stitches

are held to the back of the work. C4L also cables four stitches in total but the stitches travel to the left of the work. This may be abbreviated to C4F (cable 4 front) because the cable stitches are held at the front of the work.

With more complex cables these may show the number of stitches being moved. For example, a cable that extends over four stitches may be a 2/2 LC or a 3/1 LC. A 2/2 LC

describes two stitches held at the front of the work. A 3/1 LC has three stitches held at the front.

Special abbreviations may be shown alongside the pattern or you can refer to this glossary. Always check the abbreviations and symbols as not all designers use the same ones.

GLOSSARY OF SYMBOLS, STITCHES, AND ABBREVIATIONS

1/1 LC: Slip next stitch to cable needle and place at front of work, k1, then k1 from cable needle.

1/1 LPC: Slip next stitch to cable needle and place at front of work, p1, then k1 from cable needle.

1/1 RC: Slip next stitch to cable needle and place at back of work, k1, then k1 from cable needle.

1/1 RPC: Slip next stitch to cable needle and place at back of work, k1, then p1 from cable needle.

1/2 LC: Slip next stitch to cable needle and place at front of work, k2, then k1 from cable needle.

1/2 RC: Slip next 2 stitches to cable needle and place at back of work, k1, then k2 from cable needle.

1/2/1 LC: Slip next 4 stitches to cable needle and place at front of work, [p1, k2, p1] then p1, k2, p1 from cable needle.

1/2/1 RC: Slip next 3 stitches to cable needle and place at back of work, k1, slip 2 left-most stitches from cable needle to LH needle, move cable needle with remaining stitch to front of work, p2 from LH needle, then k1 from cable needle.

2/1 LC: Slip next 2 stitches to cable needle and place at front of work, k1, then k2 from cable needle.

2/1 LPC: Slip next 2 stitches to cable needle and place at front of work, p1, then k2 from cable needle.

2/1 RC: Slip next stitch to cable needle and place at back of work, k2, then k1 from cable needle.

2/1 RPC: Slip next stitch to cable needle and place at back of work, k2, then p1 from cable needle.

2/1/2 LC: Slip next 2 stitches to cable needle and place at front of work, slip next stitch to cable needle and place at back of work, k2, k1 from back cable needle, then k2 from front cable needle.

2/1/2 LPC: Slip next 3 stitches to cable needle and hold at front of work, k2, then slip last stitch on cable needle to LH needle, purl this stitch, then k2 from cable needle.

2/1/2 RC: Slip next 3 stitches to cable needle and place at back of work, k2, slip left-most stitch from cable needle to LH needle, move cable needle with remaining stitches to front of work, k1 from LH needle, then k2 from cable needle.

2/1/2 RPC: Slip next 3 stitches to cable needle and place at back of work, k2, slip left-most stitch from cable needle to LH needle, move cable needle with remaining stitches to front of work, p1 from LH needle, then k2 from cable needle.

GLOSSARY OF SYMBOLS, STITCHES, AND ABBREVIATIONS

2/2 LC: Slip next 2 stitches to cable needle and place at front of work, k2, then k2 from cable needle.

2/2 LPC: Slip next 2 stitches to cable needle and hold at front of work, p2, then k2 from cable needle.

2/2 RC: Slip next 2 stitches to cable needle and place at back of work, k2, then k2 from cable needle.

2/2 RCL: Slip next stitch to cable needle and place at front of work, [k1, p1] twice from cable needle.

2/2 RPC: Slip next 2 stitches to cable needle and place at back of work, p2, then k2 from cable needle.

2/2/2 LC: Slip next 2 stitches to cable needle and place at front of work, slip next 2 stitches to cable needle and place at back of work, k2, k2 from back cable needle, then k2 from front cable needle.

2/2/2 LPC: Slip next 2 stitches to cable needle and place at front of work, slip next 2 stitches to second cable needle and place at back of work, k2, p2 from back cable needle, then k2 from front cable needle.

2/2/2 RC: Slip next 4 stitches to cable needle and place at back of work, k2, slip 2 left-most stitches from cable needle to LH needle, move cable needle with remaining stitches to front of work, k2 from LH needle, then k2 from cable needle.

2/2/2 RPC: Slip next 4 stitches to cable needle and place at back of work, k2, slip 2 left-most stitches from cable needle to LH needle, move the cable needle with remaining stitches to front of work, p2 from LH needle, then k2 from cable needle.

2/3 K3togL: Slip next 2 stitches to cable needle and place at front of work, knit next 3 stitches together through back of loop (decreasing 2 stitches), then k2 from cable needle.

2/3 K3togR: Slip next 2 stitches to cable needle and place at back of work, knit next 3 stitches together through back of loop (decreasing 2 stitches), then k2 from cable needle.

2/3 LPC: Slip next 2 stitches to cable needle and place at front of work, p3, then k2 from cable needle.

2/3 RPC: Slip next 3 stitches to cable needle and place at back of work, k2, then p3 from cable needle.

3/1 LPC: Slip next 3 stitches to cable needle and place at front of work, p1, then k3 from cable needle.

3/1 RPC: Slip next stitch to cable needle and place at back of work, k3, then p1 from cable needle.

3/1/3 LPC: Slip next 3 stitches to cable needle and place at front of work, slip next stitch to second cable needle and place at back of work, k3, p1 from back cable needle, then k3 from front cable needle.

3/1/3 RPC: Slip next 4 stitches to cable needle and place at back of work, k3, slip left-most stitch from cable needle to LH needle, move cable needle with remaining stitches to front of work, p1 from LH needle, then k3 from cable needle.

3/2 LC: Slip next 3 stitches to cable needle and place at front of work, k2, then k3 from cable needle.

3/2 LPC: Slip next 3 stitches to cable needle and place at front of work, p2, then k3 from cable needle.

3/2 RC: Slip next 2 stitches to cable needle and place at back of work, k3, then k2 from cable needle.

3/2 RPC: Slip next 2 stitches to cable needle and place at back of work, k3, then p2 from cable needle.

3/3 LC: Slip next 3 stitches to cable needle and place at front of work, k3, then k3 from cable needle.

3/3 LPC: Slip next 3 stitches to cable needle and place at front of work, p3, then k3 from cable needle.

3/3 LPKP: Slip next 3 stitches to cable needle and hold at front of work, p1, k1, p1 from LH needle, then k3 from cable needle.

3/3 RC: Slip next 3 stitches to cable needle and hold at back of work, k3, then k3 from cable needle.

3/3 RPC: Slip next 3 stitches to cable needle and hold at back of work, k3, then p3 from cable needle.

3/3 RPKP: Slip next 3 stitches to cable needle and hold at back of work, p1, k1, p1 from LH needle, then k3 from cable needle.

3/3/3 SSLC: Slip next 6 stitches to cable needle and hold at front of work, k3, then move 3 stitches from the cable needle back to the LH needle, k1, p1, k1, then k3 from cable needle.

3/6 RC: Slip next 6 stitches to cable needle and hold at back of work, k3 from LH needle, then k6 from cable needle.

4/1/1 LPC: Slip next 4 stitches to cable needle and hold at front of work, k1, p1, then k4 from cable needle.

4/1/1 RPC: Slip next 2 stitches to cable needle and hold at back of work, k4, p1, then k1 from cable needle.

4/1/4 LC: Slip next 4 stitches to cable needle and place at front of work, slip next stitch to cable needle and place at back of work, k4, k1 from back cable needle, then k4 from front cable needle.

4/1/4 RC: Slip next 5 stitches to cable needle and place at back of work, k4, slip left-most stitch from cable needle to LH needle, move cable needle with remaining stitches to front of work, k1 from LH needle, then k4 from cable needle.

4/2 LPC: Slip next 4 stitches to cable needle and place at front of work, p2, then k4 from cable needle.

4/2 RPC: Slip next 2 stitches to cable needle and place at back of work, k4, then p2 from cable needle.

4/4 LC: Slip next 4 stitches to cable needle and place at front of work, k4, then k4 from cable needle.

4/4 LRC: Slip next 4 stitches to cable needle and place at front of work, [k2, p2] twice from cable needle.

4/4 RC: Slip next 4 stitches to cable needle and place at back of work, k4, then k4 from cable needle.

4/4 RCL: Slip next 4 stitches to cable needle and hold at front of work, [k1, p1] 4 times from cable needle.

4/4 RCR: Slip next 4 stitches to cable needle and hold at back of work, [k1, p1] 4 times from cable needle.

4/4 RCSS: Place next 4 stitches on cable needle and hold at back of work, k4, then [p1, k1] twice from cable needle.

4/4 RRC: Slip next 4 stitches to cable needle and place at back of work. K2, p2. K2, p2 from cable needle.

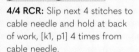

4/4 SSRC: Slip next 4 stitches to cable needle and place at back of work, [p1, k1] twice, then k4 from cable needle.

4/8 LPC: Slip next 4 stitches to cable needle and hold at front of work, p8, then k4 from cable needle.

5/5 LC: Slip next 5 stitches to cable needle and place at front of work, k5, then k5 from cable needle.

5/5 RC: Slip next 5 stitches to cable needle and place at back of work, k5, then k5 from cable needle.

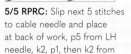

5/5 RPRC: Slip next 5 stitches to cable needle and place at back of work, p5 from LH needle, k2, p1, then k2 from cable needle.

6/6 LC: Slip next 6 stitches to cable needle and place at front of work, k6, then k6 from cable needle.

6/6 RC: Slip next 6 stitches to cable needle and place at back of work, k6, then k6 from cable needle.

6/6 RCL: Slip next 6 stitches to cable needle and place at front of work, [k1, p1] 3 times, then [k1, p1] 3 times from cable needle.

cdd, central double decrease: Slip 2 stitches together, k1, then pass slipped stitches over.

cm: Centimeter.

dec5to1, decrease 5 stitches to 1 stitch:

i) Slip next 3 stitches purlwise (as if to purl) onto RH needle.

ii) Lift second stitch on RH needle over first stitch and allow to drop off.

iii) Slip stitch from RH needle to LH needle purlwise. Lift second stitch on LH needle over first stitch and allow to drop off.

iv) Slip stitch on LH needle to RH needle.

Repeat steps ii)–iii) once more. Knit the final stitch (now on LH needle) and continue as normal (4 stitches decreased).

dec7to1, decrease 7 stitches to 1 stitch:

i) Slip next 4 stitches purlwise (as if to purl) onto RH needle.

ii) Lift second stitch on RH needle over first stitch and allow to drop off.

iii) Slip stitch from RH needle to LH needle purlwise.

iv) Lift second stitch on LH needle over first stitch and allow to drop off. Slip stitch on LH needle to RH needle.

Repeat steps ii)–iii) twice more. Knit the final stitch (now on LH needle) and continue as normal (6 stitches decreased).

in: Inch.

inc1to3, increase 1 stitch to 3 stitches: (K1, p1, k1) into the same stitch to make 3 stitches from 1.

k: knit.

ktbl, k through back loop: K next stitch through back of loop.

GLOSSARY OF SYMBOLS, STITCHES, AND ABBREVIATIONS

k2tog, knit 2 stitches together: Insert RH needle into next 2 stitches and work together as one stitch (1 stitch decreased).

k3tog, knit 3 stitches together as 1 stitch: Insert needle into next 3 stitches and k together as one (2 stitches decreased).

k3tog tbl, knit 3 stitches together through back loop: Insert needle into next 3 stitches and k together as one stitch (2 stitches decreased).

LH: Left hand.

m1, make 1 (increase 1 st): Insert LH needle from front to back under horizontal strand between LH and RH needles, knit into back of this loop.

MB, make bobble: (K1, p1, k1, p1, k1) into 1 stitch, turn, p5, turn, slip 5 stitches to RH needle purlwise, lift stitches 2, 3, 4, 5 over to leave 1 stitch.

No stitch: A stitch is decreased.

p: Purl

ptbl, purl through back loop: Purl next stitch through back of loop.

p3tog, purl 3 stitches together as 1 stitch: Insert needle into next 3 stitches and purl together as 1 stitch (2 stitches decreased).

RH: Right hand.

RS: Right side.

RS: knit

WS: purl

RS: purl

WS: knit

RS: (k1, yo, k1) in 1 stitch: Knit 1, yarn over, knit 1 in 1 stitch.

WS: (p1, yo, p1) in 1 stitch: Purl 1, yarn over, purl 1 in 1 stitch.

sl, slip: Insert RH needle into next stitch on LH needle purlwise (as if to purl). Transfer to RH needle without working the stitch.

slwyib, slip with yarn in back: Slip 1 stitch purlwise with yarn at back.

slwyif, slip with yarn in front: Slip 1 stitch purlwise with yarn in front.

sk2po, slip, knit 2 stitches together, pass slipped stitch over: Slip 1, k2tog, pass slipped stitch over.

skpo, slip, knit, pass slipped stitch over: Slip 1, k1, pass slipped stitch over.

ssk, slip, slip, knit: Slip next 2 stitches, one at a time as if to knit, to the RH needle. Insert LH needle into the fronts of these two stitches and knit them together (1 stitch decreased).

ssp, slip, slip, purl: Slip next 2 stitches one at a time as if to knit to RH needle. Purl them together, going through the back loop of the stitches.

st(s): Stitch(es).

tbl, through back loop: Insert needle into back of stitch.

wrap 4 sts: Slip 4 stitches with yarn at back, pass yarn to front, slip the 4 stitches back to the left needle, then k4 (RS)/p4 (WS).

WS: Wrong side.

⃝

yo, yarn over: Bring yarn to front of work and take over RH needle to back. Knit next stitch as normal.

* repeat instructions following asterisk as directed.

[ ] work instructions between square brackets the number of times stated.

Index

Acknowledgments

My first thank you must go to my granny, who gave me my first needles and inspired me with her amazing Fairisle and cable knitting; to the lady who took a risk on an awkward teenager, giving me my first knitting job; to the knitting magazines and, of course, to Quarto for putting their faith in my writing and designing; to my husband for his encouragement and beautiful photography; to my dear friend Julia, who gently critiques and patiently test-knits my designs—she is my knitting rock—and to my lovely family who put up with the constant clicking of needles and finding fuzzy balls of yarn stashed all over the house!

Credits

All yarns used in this book are Cascade Yarns® 220 Superwash®.
Full list of colors used is shown below.

CHAPTER ONE
365 Silver Pink
371 Chinois Green
817 Aran

CHAPTER TWO
372 Storm Cloud Heather
1961 Camel
350 Seagrass

CHAPTER THREE
1926 Doeskin Heather
1944 Westpoint Blue Heather
1942 Mint

CHAPTER FOUR
904 Colonial Blue Heather
1949 Lavender
347 Chamomile

CHAPTER FIVE
340 Dawn Pink
1946 Silver Gray
205 Purple Sage

CHAPTER SIX
349 Irish Cream
204 Smoke Blue
350 Seagrass